Security Industry Research in Singapore

Security Essentials for the 21st Century

Mr. Kenray Tan

Published By Kenray Tan

First Published 2016

ISBN 978-981-09-8205-8

CONTENTS

FOREWORD

Having been in both the private education and security industry, I took the opportunity to come up with a research on the opportunity for growth in the security industry. This research came to me during my post-graduate studies in management. Initially, my plan was to investigate a high turnover rate of a company. But radically interested in security, Special Forces, counter-terrorism and terrorism, I had eventually decided to do something related to Security. At one point, as I did an online course with Terrorism and Counter-Terrorism, I came to realize that the theory of the course consisted mainly of a mixture of history and political studies, and very little of counter-terrorism knowledge and methods. In a hard paced environment of security, not just knowing and understanding some of the history and mindsets of terrorists and their groups are good, but the need to know the practical steps to executing counter terrorism is essential. Yet, due to the low risk environment of Singapore, counter-terrorism methods are not overtly taught or addressed, except in one security course, which taught the methods through 'soft approach'. The keywords, through the 'soft approach' are: 'watch, identify, report, deter, detect and prevent'. This translates to Anti-

Terrorism. The 'hard approach' which termed as Counter-Terrorism, is usually carried out by the Special Forces, Tactical Troops and Counter-Insurgency Units. Their keywords are 'strike', 'raid' 'seek' and 'destroy'. However these keywords are not exhaustive. Perhaps, with the low to moderate risk of terrorism in Singapore, the value of security officers has not risen too far with higher end training such as 'CCTP' or 'ATO' certification, but the course of 'HCTA/RTT' under the WDA in Singapore seems sufficient at this moment. In the aspect of long working hours and harsh environment, the challenges of having to have permanent high caliber security personnel to be on duty are always there. As job become relax and less productive during the long hours, the criteria of the potential security personnel becomes lower.

In this book, instead of discussing much about terrorism and counter-terrorism, it describes briefly a few happenings of terrorism and eventually, it links to my major research in Security, the research on the opportunity for growth in the security industry in Singapore. Along the years, this research can be updated, revised, and evolved to suit new research goals and objectives. I hope you will find the book fruitful.

Kenray Tan, Author

ACKNOWLEDGEMENTS

I would like to thank my wife for helping to select the cover page photos and giving input as a reader, from a female's perspective. Without her good input, my thoughts and perspective on making this book will be limited.

I would like to thank the first publisher Mr KC Goh, for making the book a reality. Without the publisher, it would be troublesome to seek other publishers who may be able to make time to look through the manuscript and agree to print out the book at their own flexible terms and conditions.

I would like to thank my second publisher, Amazon Kindle for helping to make the republishing possible. With the availability of Amazon Kindle, I would be able to make the book relive again.

I would like to thank all readers for being interested in reading my book, especially the like-minded people in the Security industry and even current and former personnel from the forces. Also a special thank and appreciation to the non like-minded readers who are interested in reading and supporting this book.

Lastly I would like to thank myself for materializing this research into a hardcopy book, with revision and updates, and giving the will to make it happen.

INTRODUCTION

Singapore, a cosmopolitan city, has approximately 5.5 millions of people up to date. Though terrorists attack for the last 2 decades in Singapore was effectively close to none, the risk of serious crime such as murder and culpable homicide are aplenty. Fortunately, these have been handled well by the local government authorities.

Security industry is a vital industry in Singapore. It plays a significant role in protecting key installations and protecting lives and properties. It encompasses a wide plethora of execution methods and protective systems.

In the past years of terrorists attack around the globe; from Mumbai Terrorist attack (which killed over 200 people, including a Singaporean), the shooting of Sri Lanka Cricket players, the Jarkarta Ritz Carlton hotel bombing, the escaping of Mas Selamat Kestari, and the assassination of Pakistan's Lady Prime Minister Bhutto, had proven that the terrorists are getting more daring, well organized, well prepared, and well trained. The even more recent extreme cases of Paris under siege by ISIS, the beheading of a Malaysian captive by the Philipino Islamist group Abu Sayyaf, and the attacking of Mali hotel by deadly terror group Boko Haram, proves that they are all ready to be at war with humanity.

Terrorism, in fact, has blatantly become prevalent in this era. It has been made clear by the Singapore Government that the Security in Singapore should never be compromised. It cannot be lapsed, and it has to be tightened. There is no room for complacency for a small city.

What Singapore can do, is to manage the risk and deter the chance of being attack by Terrorists. Emergency preparedness and pre-emptive response has to be adequate to deal with terrorism. Through sufficient planning, drills, and preparation for readiness, the threats can be deterred and dealt with. The public should remain alert, vigilant, work hand in hand as one, and report any suspicious personnel and activities to the authority, while more highly trained security professionals are needed in the industry and in the city of Singapore.

CHAPTER ONE

SECURITY IN SINGAPORE

MANPOWER ANALYSIS AND DEMAND

The book analyses the demand for Security manpower in Singapore, and how business in the security industry thrive, in response towards deterring security threats and terrorism. The Singapore government recognizes the importance of the response through manpower as an integral part of security and counterterrorism measures. Terrorism occurs when opportunity, motivation and capability meet. Perhaps, the war against terrorism requires the elimination of at least one of the three factors, which the most crucial, as mentioned by one of the scholars, would be 'motivation'. This is because motivation often comes from ideology. The book also looks at a Singaporean's general mindset towards a Security career, which leads to the answer of current manpower crunch in Singapore, and the demand from the sector that arises, due to the crunch. The Security Regulatory had also raised the Standard of Security personnel and increases their operational capability undertaken to deter terrorism. This also helps to uplift the job to a 'better status', to a certain extent. However, this in general, would not drastically promote the career to educated young Singaporeans. Lastly, we will examine the business perspective in mind, in the Security Industry, as well as some recommendations of what more can be done to improve the operational capability and the management of the Security industry.

SECURITY JOBS ATTRACTION AND ITS CAPABILITIES

A counter-terrorism author stated in a sentence 'that in the era of prevalent terrorism around the world, an innovative multi-pronged mix of methods is needed to combat global terrorism in the young nation'. Truly, with just a small population of conscripted army and law enforcement personnel coupled and the lack of demand from Singaporeans towards a Security career, the different strengths and abilities of our community is very much needed to work hand in hand together, to augment our security capability.

In Singapore over a few decades, many young Singaporeans are becoming more educated and having higher expectation of a job nature and salary. Many young Singaporeans will most probably not consider a career as a Security Officer as it is generally perceived in their mindset to be in the nature of long hours, unproductive, and low in wages. Generally, many would have been much more qualified to take up a role with shorter working hours and higher wages in the corporate world than to take up a role as such. It would also be deemed by many, a 'temporary' or 'retired' job for them to do, if they do, or even a 'lazy' job that many would avoid.

SALARY AND PAYSCALE

Over the last decade, a part time security officer's pay has risen from a lowly $40 per 12 hours shift to up to an average of $80 per 12 hours shift now, while the gross for full time security has risen to a range of $1600 to $2300, and up to an average of $2700, for a supervisory role. However, this does not deter the fast movement and turnover for the security officers over the years. Companies need to help the industry understand that more dignity is necessary to be given to each individual security personnel. Ideally, the hours should also be shortened to at least 10 hours and below, in order to reduce fatigue level and increase motivation level, while the pay can remain around the same. But due to the constraint of controlled contract prices from clients around the nation, some of the salary scale would not be better, while the hours have to remain the same as 12 hours (taking that it would not be feasible to split each shift into 6 hours, or 8 hours plus 4 hours respectively), for clients' areas that need only 1 shift per day. The career prospect for every security personnel, such as opportunity for growth or leadership role should always be advocated, and the status of security personnel should be enhanced, and guard posts to be situated in a clean and comfortable environment. Many times, we could see guard desks placed in areas similar to a dungeon or places such as toilet areas, or dump areas behind a shopping centre.

RAISING STATUS, DIGNITY AND STANDARDS

With the rise of status and dignity in the Security industry and the re-branding of the Security industry, a person's mindset may evolve with a new impression. There should also be a group of highly elite officers who are employed to be the executive protection officers, and their capability includes being trained in martial arts, defensive driving skills, first aids, and control and restrain techniques. However, with the lack of demand of bodyguards and executive protections in Singapore, the capability and role of a security officer and protective officer often tend to overlapped each other in the private security industry.

The increase in standard by the Police Licensing Regulatory Department has placed Security officers to take up more certification courses under the 'Progressive Wage Model' scheme in the bid to enhance their capabilities and knowledge. However, the certifications still remain attractive mainly to the lower educated personnel and retirees, who are the main hallmark of the industry. It is probably that the nature and the scope of work, coupled by the need and demand of Security in Singapore, has synthesized to make the job become considerably low end, with long hours, sometimes redundant (sitting there and let time fly), therefore wages are also low.

CHAPTER TWO

SECURITY CAPABILITIES

COMMUNITY AS A KEY AGAINST TERRORISM

Given that terrorism remains a threat and crimes has taken place on a multi-faceted dimension which cannot be effectively contained merely by Law Enforcer's effort alone, more Security personnel and volunteers are therefore very much needed by organizations such as the Singapore Police Force and Singapore Civil Defence Force to add on as the auxiliary forces. However, the communities should also help to work hand in hand with the Home Team to fight emerging security concerns and not be complacent or be dependent on the government. Indeed, people and the community is the vital key to fighting terrorism. It is not possible for the government to tackle every security situations and threats alone, which is why the government had always emphasize for the community to be involved as a watch group in the deterrence and protection of lives and properties.

EXECUTIONAL CAPABILITIES

The need for the Home Team to outsource their capabilities for seaborne security, border security, prison security, has also sustained the constant need for security manpower from statutory board companies in Singapore, such as the 2 major security companies, Certis Cisco Security Pte Ltd and the Aetos Security Pte Ltd. The other popular private companies which provide security worldwide, but have a milder role in Singapore are for example G4S Security, which provides armed roles in countries around the world, and Titanium Security. Titanium security is one of the fastest growing companies providing general security services to ship security onboard vessels going overseas; they deal with piracy at seas. Titanium Security has their HQ stationed in Singapore.

KEY TARGETED AREAS AND PEOPLE DEMAND

With every corner of key targeted areas to be secured by the local law enforcement agents and their outsourced auxiliary force, there are still areas like commercial buildings and private industrial areas and estates not to be forgotten. This comes to the point where smaller private security companies come in play. With the need of key private areas to be secured, security officers are still constantly in demand. On one hand, there is a demand for security personnel to be hired by the industry; on the other hand, many educated personnel will not consider the role of security personnel as their career. This has substantiated the stronger need for manpower, and furthermore, many security officers are freelance personnel; working with a few companies to sustain their pay and salary need. Reason is that part time security officer can move around a few companies, and earn better in calculating their total wages proportion, as compared to a full time security officer. But in most recent regulation stated by the Police Licensing Division, security personnel can only join up to a maximum of 2 security agencies.

RESEARCH OBJECTIVES

This book evaluates the opportunity for growth in the Security Industry in Singapore.

The 5 objectives are stated as below:

- To evaluate the opportunity for growth in for Security Industry in Singapore.

- To understand a person's preference and mindset in considering a career in the security industry.

- To analyze the demand of security professionals to be hired in Singapore, in lieu of prevalent terrorism around the world.

- To study whether the tightening of standard by the Police Licensing Regulatory Department has improved the standard of the security professionals to effectively handle security and counter-terrorism situation.

- Added on materials to introduce some basic essentials needed to protect one in times of needs.

CHAPTER THREE

TERRORISM THREATS

SINGAPORE

Singapore, a cosmopolitan city, has approximately 5.5 millions of people up to date. Though terrorists attack for the past 2 decades in Singapore was effectively close to none, the global threats of recent Terrorism are real and close. Despite the good handling and preparation against imminent threats by the authorities of Singapore, the local government's proposal of close to 6.9 million citizenships in the next decade would inevitable tint Singapore's safety and security, amid other problems such as cleanliness and congestion, which will not come into the picture of this book.

WAR AGAINST HUMANITY

In almost a decade ago of terrorist attacks; from Mumbai Terrorist attack (which killed over 200 people, including a Singaporean), the shooting of Sri Lanka Cricket players, the Jarkarta Ritz Carlton hotel bombing, the escaping of Mas Selamat Kestari, and the assassination of Pakistan's Lady Prime Minister Bhutto, had proved that the terrorists are getting more daring, well organized, and well trained. They are also better funded to be able to equip themselves.

In the recent years on the US war on Terrorism (The killing of Osama Bin Laden), Bali on high alert after tip off on attack for his inaugural 10 years commemoration of the Island's first blast, and the crippling of Jemaah Islamiyah Terrorist Group (by the effective Indonesian Forces), had not lowered down the guard of counter-terrorism in the respective countries. The crippling of Terrorist groups and killing of Osama, which links to the Al-Qaeda group, will somehow mean revenge from the latter and/or other Terrorist groups. This had came closely true, with the even more recent extreme cases of Paris under siege by ISIS, the beheading of a Malaysian captive by the Philipino Islamist group Abu Sayyaf, and the attacking of Mali hotel by deadly terror group Boko Haram, had proven that the terror groups are all ready to be at war with humanity. These had constantly increased the red alert of security in Singapore, preparing it for any strikes when necessary.

MONITORING GLOBAL THREATS

The significant and imperative situation is to monitor the major global issues revolving around the world and guard against the global threats. Terrorism, in fact, has blatantly become prevalent in this era. It has been made clear by the Singapore Government that Security in Singapore should never be compromised. It cannot be lapsed, and it has to be tightened. There is no room for complacency in this little red dot. Amongst those mentioned above, Terrorism continues to prevail in countries in the Middle East, Europe and U.S, and effort to combating them is still on-going.

In relation to Terrorist threats around the world, the topics gear towards the local context of Singapore. It should be of interest to security owners and managers, as well as all security personnel and anyone who are literate and able to appreciate and understand the research at a higher level. It evaluates the opportunity for growth in the Security Industry; the analysis of the need to hire more Security Professionals in Singapore, and the professional standard of the Security Personnel. The main body of the section looks into the security industry and its development in Singapore, and information related to task and readiness, which the opportunity for growth can be evaluated through some of the articles, followed by conclusion. Bonus materials such as traits, skills, and procedure to handle security threats will also be included in the book.

THE DEFENCE AND COUNTER–INSURGENCY

Countries can manage the risk and deter the chance of being attack by terrorism. This includes Singapore. There is no adequate replacement for emergency preparedness and pre-emptive response, as the word 'always be ready' strikes ones' mind as a Singaporean. The most assured way of deterring and dealing with a threat and reacting effectively, is through adequate planning and training for readiness. Indeed, the total defence serves as unity for all defence from social to economic defence. In the physical way to defend, combat readiness of national servicemen and army regulars will serve to defend Singapore in war situations, while the Elite Special Operation

Task Force has been created to physically combat terrorism and insurgency both locally and globally. The belief that the Special Operation Task Force (made up of the elite Diver units and the Special Operation Force Troopers from the Commandos Formation), are the breed of men trained and ready to take down these perpetrators anytime, while the Special Operations Command Troopers will be the first responder to deal with homeland threats such as riots, hostage situations, and terrorism attack within the home ground. Lastly, before all physical actions are being executed, the counter-intelligence unit has to provide the vital information and intelligence for executions.

CHAPTER FOUR

THE SECURITY WORKFORCE

ENTICING MATURE CANDIDATES

In the last few years, the Workforce Development Agency and Singapore's Police Licensing and Regulatory Department had launched a project called 'Project Silver Lining'. This project is to offer shorter working hours to attract mature candidates back to the workforce. This is to meet the current shortfall of some 30 percent of security officers needed in the industry. Despite the shorter working hours offered, many security companies have perpetually offer 12 hours posts, which includes the Auxiliary Police Force. The attraction to offer shorter working hours may only serves to attract and cajole mature candidates back to the workforce to contribute to the society, but more could be done for other age groups. Despite the project to offer shorter working hours, the long working hours of a 12 hours shift is indeed, still widely spread across the nation and is current.

OVERHAULING THE INDUSTRY

Security industry in Singapore needs to make good changes if it wants to address the endemic problems like the shortage of manpower and the low expertise level. Changes may include having management process to be more in line with those other industries; pushing for shorter work hours, and using of technology so that staff could be better deployed. However, a lot of solutions such as pushing for shorter hours and leveraging the use of technology is idealistic, and is not of immediate solution to the problem. This is due to costing and the needs from clients. Pushing for shorter hours may means segregation of timing and hiring of more manpower which will create another challenge of having to find more people which will result in an even greater shortfall, and the difference in proportion of paying more in total to more people, while the costing to clients may increase substantially which will pose a challenge to the clients and agencies alike, therefore it will take longer research to cure the situation.

MANAGEMENT AND HIRING OF MANAGERS

One major problems faced by the industry is the uneven level of management expertise. It is said that the management capabilities are lacking when compared to other sectors. Security firms often hire middle managers who do not always possess sufficient supervisory skills. Some of the management problem, for instance is the poor management of welfare to employees, as well as being reactive and unprepared for worst case security scenarios. With this, the first way to identify the gaps of these managers and to bridge it is to advocate a training course for them, most relevant to their training needs. Of course, it is not all foolproof. With the training knowledge equipped, the managers would be able to increase their thinking in higher order, and able to make better judgment, as compared to no training.

One of the industry practitioner stated that we need to look for people with real supervisory and management abilities from any other industry who can plan and come up with good procedures for security operations, and that people with real supervisory and management abilities comes from both education and soft skills'. But to me, it would be a chance of 50/50 to hire such person, as people with substantial skills of both tend not to be attracted to the security industry, but it is not all hopeless. An alternative management and supervisory skills comes from former regulars (senior officers) from the SPF or SAF, which is the next viable decision.

SECURITY CONVERSIONS

In a security conference years ago, the Singapore Workforce Development Agency has announced two new security conversion programmes to train security officers and supervisors. Under the two programmes, WDA co funds 90 percent of the course to train mid career hires, with 10 percent bonded by the employers. Indeed, the announcement comes in timely, and it is good to certify a potential person to be an eligible security officer. But more could be done, such as prestige and pay must be factored in. If prestige is increased, more people with higher education may join as high end Protective officer. But despite the lack of industry demand due to the low to moderate risk in Singapore, Security and Protection personnel are not highly appreciated, therefore the productiveness is also not significant, which answer the reason why the wages are not attractive.

SECURITY RECRUITMENT

The search for manpower has also led some firms to come up with new recruitment strategies less common in the industry. These include hiring women with flexible work arrangement, as women make up about 12 to 15 percent of the industry's 35 000 strong workforce. However, there are some practitioners who feel the shorter working hours may not work for everyone due to the manpower crunch and the higher cost which clients might not want to pay for. The 12 hours work day is the specific problem which has been a long standing issue and deterrent to attract people into the industry. One example is a firm who placed a recruitment advertisement for a 12 hours shift, which got the most 5 applicants a day. But when the advertisement comes with a six to eight hour job, the firm got a beeline of about 200 people within 3 days. Unwaveringly, the

12 hours shift is still prevalent across the nation and in the present year 2015. Despite the long hours, it is a long standing issue that is not to be solved overtime.

INCENTIVES FOR JOINING THE AUXILIARY POLICE FORCE

The Auxiliary Police Force, in the bid to attract more talents to join their security force, offers cash bonuses and extra perks such as free attraction tickets and transport concessions. They are giving carrots to get younger people the join the industry.

In my opinion, Armed security companies are dangling carrots to lure young people to join the industry, especially offering high monetary bonuses to experienced officers-to-be. In 2013, Certis Cisco had offered up to 12 thousand dollars joining bonus while Aetos had offering 10 thousand dollars joining bonus. Certis Cisco is also offering scheme for A'level/Diploma holders to join them as a regular Sergeant, comparable to the Singapore Police Force. However, the not so good news would be that if anyone has higher qualification other than what they can offer, the potential person will only be offered what the company can only offer maximum. This will be the limitation to a potential participant. Unless one is a commissioned officer previously in the Army/Police, then Certis Cisco may be able to hire the participant as a minimum rank of 'Inspector'.

CHAPTER FIVE

SECURITY & COUNTER-TERRORISM

SECURING OUR BORDER

Beside conventional firearms, knife killings and explosive devices, Terrorists are also leveraging the use of biological, radiological, chemical agent and cyber warfare to execute terrorism. To stay ahead of the threats, Singapore needs to share their strategies and learn from other countries as well. As a non airtight country, it is imperative for us to detect and stop any threat as far away from our borders as possible. This starts from strengthening the borders as it is the first line of defence at top priority. The manpower is always necessary. In fact, the more manpower, the merrier. Fortunately, the current situation is still in control, with adequate manpower to protect the front with the current threat level.

LONE/DIY TERRORIST

In recent year, experts noticed a worrying tend of individuals who are taking up personal extremist causes and launching violent attack on their own. While these self radicalized individuals are typically "converted" to the terrorist cause mainly by using online research, many also listen to radical ideologues to become the 'mujahidin'. Some have been tempted to join terrorist camps in Pakistan, Afghanistan, and Syria, have taken active steps to sign up for jihadist training. Internet has played its roles of having the ease of access and communication, where it becomes a popular platform for recruiting and converting people. An example is that Al-Qaeda posts its leaders' sermon online and has been known to recruit people through online chat rooms and social networking. In the matter not detectable among the midst, as long as significant threat is not being found, and there is no evidence of imminent plot, it is not easy to sole define if one is genuinely planning to harm the country for its cause.

FACING OFF FUTURE THREATS

Threats from lone wolves and small splinter terrorist cells may prove more dangerous as most of these home-grown Terrorist are more proficient in going about their business undetected by blending into the community. The harder part would be there law enforcement agencies would not be able to detect them as they do not have criminal or security records and authorities may also lack resources to follow up on every suspected individual. Base on the article, I think this could be truly challenging, however, lone wolves can be succumbed on the spot during crisis negotiation stage, and be intercepted, if being detected. But it is hopeful that justice can be brought to the lone wolves to prevent subsequent tasks. In this aspect, I would sometimes address the lone wolves and small splinter terrorists as 'criminals', 'assailants' or 'perpetrators', rather than pure 'terrorists'. If they have no links to organization, they will most likely be barred under criminal act rather than terrorism.

SINGAPORE'S EXPERIENCE WITH TERRORISM

Singapore came under Terrorism attack in late 1987, targeted the American International Assurance building and shell tower. Before 1987, it came under a number of other small-scale bombing, some which involved Palestinians. In 1991, the Singapore Counter-Terrorism Unit received international attention when it successfully stormed a hijacked airliner and killed four Terrorists claiming to be members of the Pakistan People's Party. Terrorist violence in Singapore then diminished after 1991. Months after the 9/11 attacks, the threat of terrorism returned. Singapore's Internal Security Department (ISD) deterred the JI branch from launching a series of bomb attacks targeting foreign embassies and U.S interests in the country in December 2011. In regards to the article, the current moment in Singapore is that no plot(s) is/are to be uncovered so far. However, readiness is always in the balls and the forces take matter seriously.

SECURING SINGAPORE

Singapore has managed to ward off all terrorism since the first JI arrest in the last decade, even though it has been targeted in several known ploys. As at late 2011, the Internal Security Department was still holding 16 men in detention for terrorist activities and another 46 were on restriction orders or suspension directions. The ISD has also successfully arrested more than 10 Singaporean JI members from overseas due to intelligence provided by the ISD. Through various measures implemented after 2001, the nation has significantly made itself 'infertile' for terrorists. However, the country is still a prime target for attacks, especially from terrorist groups in the neighboring countries. One of the Singapore's common strategy of advocating the community to come together as one, to watch and report any irregularities to deter and mitigate terrorism seems to be effective. However, it has yet to be tested. Generally, many scholars believe that Singapore is able to deal with the situation well, should the need arises.

STRENGTHENING CRISIS MANAGEMENT CAPABILITIES

In the crisis situation, it is paramount to maintain public confidence in the government. This will help prevent stress and give the government the necessary time and space to execute measures against the crisis. Media and the correct use of words are also crucial to addressing the public. In achieving this, the MHA has put in place a Home-front Crisis Management System (HCMS) to ensure government agencies can respond quickly and effectively in times of an attack. Although the above system by MHA is not often heard of, it is believe that it has a vital role to play towards response in crisis and will bring about the best to counter the attack.

LIAISING WITH BUSINESS TO ENHANCE SECURITY

The police force website stated that businesses can make a significant contribution to the national security as well. The Safety and Security Watch Group (SSWG) extends the CSSP idea to businesses and commercial buildings within a geographical area. Companies within the same area can come together and form a committee to look into security issues facing the area. There are currently more than 120 such groups covering more than 900 building across the country. In the same string, an Industry safety and Security Watch Group (iSSWG) bring companies from the same industry together to deal with security issues unique to their industry. In this, I would think that it has comprehensively help industry and companies to come up together to deal with the issue. However, more could be done, such as implementing an individual volunteering watch group, and also make the security neighborhood watch group more readily available and prominent to the community, and advocate the volunteerism on it.

THE WHOLE OF GOVERNMENT PLATFORM

Government has spent much resources and energy and has played the whole-of-government approach as a key role in the counter-terrorism efforts. While the whole-of-government platform forms a strong basis for dealing with the threats thrown up by a complex and inter-related global threat, the involvement of private and public sector is also proving to be crucial in ensuring a vigorous response against a terrorism threat. Private and community organizations, including businesses, have a key role in securing the nation. The government has thus devoted substantial resources to help businesses upgrade their security features and implement strong continuity plans. I concurred that adopting the measures can help provide companies with key competitive edge in a volatile global business environment, and help them reap business benefits that go beyond the initial cost they paid to invest in security.

INDUSTRY GROWTH

Years ago, a WDA article mentioned that security industry comprises over 270 Security agencies. The sector is projected to grow at a rate of 3 to 5 % yearly, in tandem with the projected growth of the economy in Singapore. The positions include security officers, protections officers, enforcement officers, auxiliary police officers, and many more. At present, WDA have also offered Framework and competency courses to security personnel following their years of working experience, to increase their competency level, and to attain their rank and pay scale upon the completion of the required module(s). This is currently supported by the Union and offer under the Progressive Wage Model.

THE NEXT LAP

More than a decade after the first Jemaah Islamiyah (JI) arrests were made in Singapore, the country has staved off any attack from terrorism. The global threat landscape has however, continue to evolve rapidly. The emerging issues continue. There are newer technology and advanced equipment as well as more efficient and coordination system boosted on the war against terrorism. However, warding off the ill intentions of the extremists boil down to one simple key element, which is the Human factor. While it was important to invest in technology and put forth the best security systems, it is the people on the ground - The frontline security officers as well as the public, whom collectively, play the biggest role in deterring attacks.

An example would be a former Pakistani President Pervez Musharraf was saved from an assassination attempt by militants because of his two quick-thinking frontline personnel. One was a police officer who spotted a suspicious car at gas station and approached the car, scaring the terrorist to detonate his device prematurely, while the other, who is the President's driver, kept his cool and managed to drive off, avoiding being trapped in the convoy. Both men saved the president's life by their simple actions, which can thwart the terrorist's plan.

With these, the human factor can be seen to be a boon or bane in Security, depending on the front-liners' wit and reaction, which is critical to the efficacy of any security regime. As felt, if one is vigilant, thinking and empowered officer, a competent person who knows his terrain, the chances of a threat being detected are reasonable high.

WRAPPING UP

The Security industry in Singapore is very much in demand and the consistent need for manpower is necessary in order to play an integral role in maintain the overall security of Singapore. The need to secure Singapore against Terrorism plays a constant and never ending mission. The need for manpower will still be necessary to counter all these threats. The current situation for manpower is leveraging the use of neighbouring foreign talents such as Malaysians and local senior citizens. However, more needs to be done to increase the prestige for the job sector. In responding to the challenges, various methods have been tried by industry players, yet movement is still dim. The Singapore governing is also continuing forward with proactive measures to cope with emerging terrorist threats, which one of the measures is to increase the use of manpower, which will nevertheless be necessary.

CHAPTER SIX

SECURITY RESEARCH & METHODOLOGY

INTRODUCTION

In this chapter, the methods of study and research to achieve the goals of this book will be discussed. The overall range of the various research mode and approaches will be introduced.

To narrow down to the objectives, the most viable methods for this field work will be selected and justified for implementation. Lastly, the strength and limitation of the research process will also be described in this chapter. This chapter will look very much into the methodology implementation with minimal description of security and counter-terrorism issues.

RESEARCH

Research can be defined as a scientific and systematic search for relevant information on a specific topic. Under the Advanced Learner's Dictionary, it stated that 'Research is an art of scientific investigation'. 2 writers, Redman and Mory in the 1920s defined research as a systematized effort to gain new knowledge. Some consider research as a movement from the known to the unknown, or even a voyage of discovery. Research is an academic activity. According to a writer Clifford Woody in the 1950s, research comprises of hypothesis or suggested solutions, collecting, organizing, and evaluating data, making logical inference and reaching a conclusion, and finally, to evaluate a conclusion to determine whether they fit the formulated findings. Research is thus, an original contribution to the existing stock of knowledge. The search for knowledge through objective and a systematic way of finding solutions to a problem is research. The approach concerning generalization and the formulation of new theory is also call research, as such. The term 'Research' can be referred to the systematic method.

RESEARCH APPROACHES

There are two approaches to my research, one is quantitative, and the other, qualitative. The former involves the generation of data in quantitative form which can be subjected to quantitative analysis in a systematic fashion. This can be further broken down into inferential, experimental, and simulation approaches to research. The purpose for inferential approach to research is to form a data to infer characteristics or relationships of population. This commonly means survey research where a sample of population is studied to determine its characteristics and then inferred that the population has the same characteristics.

Experimental approach is characterized by a more controlled research environment, and in this case are variables are manipulated to observe their effects on the other variables.

Simulation approach involves the construction of a simulated environment within which relevant information and data can be generated. This allows observation of the active behaviour of a system under controlled conditions. The 'simulation' term, to the context of business refers to 'the operation of a numerical model that represents the structure of a dynamic process'. Simulation is also run to represent the behaviour of the process over time, over the given values of conditions, parameters and exogenous variables. It is also useful in building models for understanding future conditions.

Qualitative approach to research is linked with individual assessment of opinions, behaviour, and attitudes. Research in this kind of situation is a function of researcher's insights and impressions. Such an approach to research generates results either in non-quantitative form or in ways not subjected to rigorous quantitative analysis. Generally, the technique of focus group, in-depth interviews, and projective techniques are used.

RESEARCH METHODS AND TECHNIQUES

Some possible type of research techniques listed below:

Library – Analysis of historical recording of notes, content analysis, tape and film listening, and research record analysis.

Analysis of documents – Statistical complications and manipulations, reference, and abstract guides, contents analysis.

Field – Non-participant direct observation behavioural scales, use of score cards, research observations etc.

Participant Observation – Interactional recording, tape recorders, photographic techniques etc.

Mass Observation – Recording mass behaviour, interview using independent observers in public places.

Mail questionnaire - Identification of social and economic background of respondents.

Questionnaire – Use of attitude scales, projective techniques, use of socio-metric scales.

Personal interview – Interviewer uses a detailed schedule with open and closed questions.

Focused interview – Interviewer focuses attention upon a given experience and its effects

Group interview – Small groups of respondents are being interviewed simultaneously.

Telephone survey – Used as a survey tool for information and for discerning opinion.

Laboratory – Small group study of random use of audio-visual recording devices, use of observers, research behaviour, play, and role analysis.

RESEARCH DESIGN

After defining the research method, the next section will discuss the implementation of it. The below will introduce the design methods, respondents, and sampling taken from the research methods such as in-depth interviews and questionnaire surveys. In the research method for the 4 of the 5 objectives, a structured questionnaire, which consist mainly close-ended questions will reach the wide public of age range around 18 to 60, to find out about one's mindset in considering a career in the security industry. The total questions for this quantitative approach will be 12 unstructured questions, as the outcome will perceived to be accurate and not restrictive to the exhibition of users' flow of opinions. The in-depth interview will be crafted such that all 8 questions are open-ended and generally structured. This helps to find out from 4 industry players and opinion leaders, their views on the demand of security professionals to be hired in Singapore. Lastly, all information will be garnered for analysis.

RESPONDENTS FOR THE INTERVIEWS

In qualitative data research, the respondents of the in-depth interviews are people from the security or military industry who have extensive experience and knowledge in their field. Thus, the security personnel, security manager, counter-terrorism personnel or Auxiliary Police personnel are the appropriate respondents. Four of the security related personnel will be involved in the samplings for the in-depth interviews. The interview will begin with an open-ended question of the demand of security profession needed in Singapore, followed by the rest of the other questions. This addresses the research objective 1, 2, 3 and 4, which is on the demand of the professional needed in Singapore, the growth opportunity; the understanding on whether the tightening of standard by the PLRD does help improved the standard of the security professionals.

In the quantitative data research, objective 2 is mainly addressed to understand a person's preference and mindset in considering a career in the security industry, coupled with some questions from objective 1, 3, and 4. This research will go by questionnaire-survey to target to a public profile of 18 to 60 of age.

IN–DEPTH INTERVIEWS

The in-depth interview is an 8 qualitative structured interview questions gearing towards opinion leaders and players who are relevant to the industry. This is to investigate the demand of security personnel needed in the industry, and whether the tightening of the standard for security personnel has indeed increased the standard of security personnel in totality. It also helps to garner their views on what normal young people who are educated, think and feel about considering a career in the security industry, namely targeted to a lower skilled position, such as a security guard/officer etc.

QUANTITATIVE SURVEY

In garnering quantitative data, survey is the main tools to use for the research mainly on objective number 2. It needs to be structured in the direction of general preference of a person's choice towards a security profession given by their educational background, their age, and the nature of the job etc.

Comprehensively, their opinions were also sought after, for other objectives in 1, 3, and 4. The targeted respondents are a general public from 18 to 60 of age, whereby the general perception of the role of the position from the civilians are very much needed for analysis.

THE AIMS OF THE QUESTIONAIRE

A. <u>First person standing role</u>

A total of 1 rating question to simulate an imagine of one standing as a security guard, with 5 points, and rating of 1 to 5 for preference aimed to investigate the previous working remuneration, job satisfaction, working hours, the status of the security work and whether it can attract different age groups and profiles of the public.

B. <u>Job demand</u>

A total of 3 questions and aim is to explore the local expectations towards their preferred job.

C. <u>Perception of the job</u>

A total of 4 questions aim to examine the local perception and mindset towards a security job.

D. <u>Improved Capabilities</u>

A total of 4 questions aim to find out if the existing recommendations for improvised skills in officer will be vital to the Security industry to attract more manpower in the industry.

E. <u>Personal profile</u>

The personal details of the survey takers will be use for collation and profiling purposes. The personal information can be used to generate analysis on their thoughts and thinking base on the different group of profiles being categorized together accordingly.

ETHICAL ISSUES

In research, ethical issues are the inevitable issues one should have considered before the research. The survey will tend to collect sensitive information from respondents, such as name, age, gender, education background. However, with the data protection regulation and for the protection of every individual respondent, the options will be included for respondents to choose if they are fine to share information, before the start of the survey. The researcher must ensure that all the information collected will be in confidence all time. This is for the quantitative data.

In the in-depth interview, participants will be asked if it is fine for them to share their information with the public when publishing their opinions, before the start of the interview. This is because the collected qualitative data will be more sensitive and needed to be published; therefore permission to seek to reveal the interviewee's information will be necessary. The researcher will have to make known to the respondents and interviewees that they have the right to use and publish all the collected information when garnering the date for research.

LIMITATIONS OF THE RESEARCH PROCESS

In the limitation, due to the sole capacity of the researcher (myself) and with the limited time given to conduct the survey, interviews and fieldwork, the sampling size will be relative small. The small number of respondents and interviewees may affect the reliability and precision of the research outcome, but fortunately, as the interviewees for the interviews are the industry players and opinion leader, they could almost represent some majority of the security personnel in the industry, as most of them share similar views, experiences, and exposure. Their opinions can only be differentiated and affected by their inborn personality, but the gist of their opinions will be able to adequately address the majority's opinion in the security industry. The last minor problem would be the researcher's limited skills and expertise in conducting the surveys and interviews, and the lack of skills in the data analytical software may contribute to less expertise in the presentation of the data findings.

CHAPTER SEVEN

FINDINGS AND ANALYSIS

INTRODUCTION

Further to the preceding chapter on the research methodology, this chapter covers the discussions and simple presentations of the collected data and information. It encompasses the respondent's profile, the findings garnered from the interviews and surveys, as well as the empirical analysis of the findings. For identification protection, the actual profile and info of the respondents will not be revealed.

RESPONDENT'S PROFILE IN THE IN–DEPTH INTERVIEW

On collecting qualitative data for the research, three industry players have been invited for the in-depth interviews in 2013 and re-contacted for update of their views. The details of the 3 respondents are as follow:

Name:	RESPONDENT 1	RESPONDENT 2	RESPONDENT 3
Age:	36	43	43
Gender:	Male	Male	Male
Education:	Secondary	Adv. Cert in Security Operation	Bachelor Degree
Occupation:	Former Protection Officer	Auxiliary Police	Self-Defence Instructor
Company:	XXXXXX	XXXXXX	XXXXXX
Interview Locality:	MBS	Mcdonald	Safra

RESEARCH FINDINGS

The portion below will discuss the findings from both the in-depth interviews with the industry players and surveys from the perception of the public.

FINDINGS IN THE STRUCTURED IN-DEPTH INTERVIEWS

Respondent 1 - XXXXX, Former Protection Supervisor:

The security industry is constantly in demand of manpower, due to the fact that security is imperative in all countries, and human beings cannot take for granted in this. In the society, many places like the commercial buildings to government buildings need security to look after their lives and property, and to ensure that things are in order. The tightening of standard by the PLRD over the years have improved the standard of the physical security professional to effectively handle security and counter-terrorism situation to some extent, as more officers needs to be certified 'competent' in their area of work before being deployed, as compared to the previous time, where non-trained personnel can be deployed anytime. However, no matter which industry it is, there is always room for improvement and by tightening the standard; it reflects the professionalism in the people doing the job.

Young Singaporeans will only consider security as a job, due to reasons like interest in short term, for pocket money, during their studies or vacation. With the increases in demand for these events and ad-hoc security, part time security scheme is being introduced to entice people in short term. Young local may also consider a career only if they are really unable to secure a good job or career in their area of scope or interest, and for those formerly from various uniform groups, it is an exception for them to be in consideration for a career in the security. The only thing to keep abreast is to upgrade their skills by constantly taking up a security relevant course or workshop.

The things that hinder local young Singaporeans to consider a career in the security industry, like any other industry, are due to various reasons and factors that one could actually thought of. In the nature of a security job, it would definitely create some stress due to the scope of the tasks, the general low pay, and the long working hours enough for both sitting and standing, which to some, the focus power is affected.

In things pertaining to promoting security jobs to young educated Singaporeans from Diploma and above to consider a career in the industry, security industry, like most service industries, the job has the least amount of respect given in terms of job nature and various reasons such as stress created at work, low pay in general, long working hours, and the losing of concentration, which also in turn, affects the vigilance of the job requirement. There is always room for improvements like better pay, shorter working hours, increasing prestige given to the job, and enhanced capability to be widen.

Respondent 2 - XXXXX, Auxiliary Police Officer:

The security industry is constantly in demand of manpower due to the fact that there are tremendous requirements for part time officers, and for the buffering of the reliefs. The part time Auxiliary Police Officer scheme was also introduced years ago, but restricted to certain groups such as those who were once an armed uniformed personnel in the SPF and SAF. The tightening of standard by the PLRD over the years has nevertheless improved the standard of the security professional, as to better prepare the officers for worst case scenarios, and to inculcate to all officers that there should never be complacency in handling security issues. In general, local young educated Singaporeans may still consider a career in the security industry, especially in the Auxiliary Police Force, due to the introduction of the scheme for Diploma/A'level holders, and the attraction of certain perks, such as joining bonuses of up to 12 thousand dollars previously, and current 5 thousand dollars, amid other on-going variable components. There are also progressions in certain specialized sector within the force, therefore ultimately, young Singaporeans may still consider.

Generally, especially to the Unarmed Security Industry, the things that hinder local young Singaporeans would be no progression, or little progression, and getting stagnated until a certain point will be the consideration deterring them to consider the career. The most important things to promote the industry to young educated Singaporeans is a well planned career path way and progression (especially in rank), and higher responsibility for them. This has to be made known transparently to the public, and for the awareness of the public.

The Security films in Singapore could have at least a couple of people who are highly experienced and trained in the management of a business, so that they could sustain and improve the business according to the needs of the economy. It is also good to get management people from other sectors, but the people must have a keen interest in security; otherwise, they would have brought in just a narrow perspective from their previous industry, which may not work in the security industry.

For the sake of stability and recognition, a better remuneration package, shorter working hours, stronger management in the business, branding of the organization and prestige built on the organization and the status of security personnel would help enhance the security business.

Respondent 3 - XXXXXX Security Self-Defence Instructor:

The Security industry is constantly in demand of manpower; this is due to the perceived low status and low salary that security officers get. It is not able to retain young people and often, the industry can mostly get the elderly or retired to work. Turnover rate is usually quite high and job satisfaction is low.

Generally, local young Singaporeans will not consider a career in the Security Industry. This is due to the high level and cost of living in Singapore, which it is still safe to choose the better paying paths over the lower skilled and higher risk jobs in the security industry. However, there are also the minority of the people who do choose this path due to their interest in security and counter-terrorism. The lack of status is another factor. Young local people do not like to be looked down upon by fellow peers when it comes to a career choice.

The main factors that hinder local young Singaporeans to consider a career in the security industry would be the low salary, low status, and the uncertainty of where the job will lead to in one's career. With this, the reasonable improvement of salary to match other industry, and the accelerated status of the job, may promote the career to young educated Singaporeans with Diploma and above.

The Security films in Singapore to have at least a couple of people who are highly experience in the management of a business, would be preferred by more often than not, as they run on lower budget and competition can be a cut throat, therefore it is good to have people who are strong in the management of a business to help enhance the overall security business.

A better remuneration package, shorter hours provided, and stronger management, branding and prestige built over the security film helps enhance the security business is agreeable, because these are the very main reasons that people, especially the local young Singaporean will choose to be a security officer, if the above factors mentioned are achieved in due time.

RESPONDENTS FOR THE CLOSE ENDED SURVEY

The respondents of the questionnaire surveys are general public age 21 to 45, local Singaporeans or permanent residents. Most of them are generation X and Y males and females. While the older age respondents consist of 1/3 of the total respondents. The education level of the respondents varies, however their perceptions are in general, similar and pretty conclusive. The actual number of participants for the survey was 115; however, only 110 of them have successfully filled up the survey legibly.

FINDINGS FROM THE CLOSE ENDED SURVEYS

The findings generated in simple percentages of the surveys (but without empirical analysis) can be stated and concluded as it is, as followed. Please note that it does not denote any analysis or conclusion, but just a presentation of paragraphs of the percentage details:

PART A: MINDSETS OF CIVILIANS ON A ROLE OF A SECURITY OFFICER/GUARD

The survey results in questions indicated that 63% felt that the salary of a Security Officer/Guard is the most dislike by the civilians, while 37% felt neutral on it. In terms of working conditions, such as the average working hours of 10 to 12 hours, 9% felt 'okay' with the hours, while 19% as neutral, the rest of the 72% felt that the working hours is too long and tiring. In terms of job status, 55% felt the job status as neutral, while 45% felt that the job status is what they dislike. In terms of productivity, 36% felt neutral with it, while 64% of the people felt that it is not very productive n general. In the question of redundancy of the job, 36% felt that a security's job is redundant to have, while 64% felt it is imperative. In question 6, 27% felt neutral about the security job as redundant, while 73% disagree to strongly disagree. On feeling unproductive in doing the job, 23% express strongly agree to agree, while 27% is neutral, and the remaining 50% felt disagree to strongly disagree, and they find that the job cannot be said as unproductive. On the job perception of being embarrassed, 36% felt neutral, while 64% rated disagree to strongly disagree on the embarrassment part. In terms of low skilled in nature, 37% agreed to it, while 27% are neutral. 36% goes with disagree to strongly disagree. In the question of being asked on imagining the role as a standing security officer being redundant, 27% goes with strongly agree to agree, while 18% goes with neutral. Ironically, the last 55% goes with disagree to strongly disagree that the role of a standing officer is redundant. On being unproductive, 18% goes with strongly agree, while 27% are neutral. 55% goes with disagree to strongly disagree. In terms of feeling low skilled in nature,

45% goes with strongly agree to agree, while 18% goes with neutral; while 36% goes with disagree to strongly disagree.

PART B: OPPORTUNITY FOR GROWTH, DEMAND, AND IMPROVEMENT

In the question of sustainability, 81% felt that the business is sustainable, while 19% goes with neutral. In the question of improvement, 73% strongly felt that the security industry in Singapore has the potential opportunity to improve, while 27% do not think so. In question on the need for more manpower, 91% of the participants strongly agree to agree that despite the prevalent terrorism attacks around the world, Singapore will need a good number of Security manpower to safeguard the residential and commercial buildings alike, while 9% disagree. In the question on the hiring and outsourcing needs for physical security, the industry in Singapore will have the opportunity for growth in the coming years, 73% goes with agree to strongly agree, while 9% goes with neutral, and 19% disagree.

PART C: EFFECTIVENESS OF THE TIGHTENING OF STANDARD

In the question on the view of enhancing the capabilities with self-defence skills, 82% of the people agree to strongly agree, while 18% goes with disagree to strongly disagree. For the same question on the view of self-defence skills, the 82% who strongly agree to agree, had chosen 5 choices of the self-defence skills for the security personnel. Of choices selected, only 3.9% goes with Karate, while 11% goes with Taekwondo. 7.4% goes with Muay Thai, while 29.6% goes with the Israeli Military Forces Self-Defence. 22.2% goes with Mixed Martial Arts, while 14.8% goes with Wing Chun Close combat martial arts. The last 11.1% goes with Judo. For the question applicable to those who disagree with having self-defence skills for security personnel, the 18% who disagree that a security officer/guard should have the capability of self-defence skill, 9% felt that the security officers/guards main task is to watch, deter and report, therefore there is no need for self-defence, while another 9% felt that most security officers may not be physically fit enough to be trained in self-defence. In the question on Police Licensing Regulatory Department has made known that self-defence training is not necessary to be acquired by Security Officers/Guards, as their main role is only to watch, deter, and report when necessary, only 18% of the public had agreed, while the rest of the 82% of the public participant had disagreed.

PART D: PARTICIPANTS' PROFILE

Of the 110 participants, 73% of the respondents are males, while 27% are females. In addition, 64% of the respondent age groups were between 31 to 45 years, while the last 36% falls between 21 to 30 years. In educational level, 27% of the respondents have a Masters degree, while 45% holds a Bachelor degree. 10% holds a diploma, while the last 18% holds secondary level to NITEC level.

ANALYSIS OF THE IN-DEPTH INTERVIEW

This part will analyze the findings of the in-depth interviews. However, due to a revision, one of the three industry players who has taken up the interview has a question lesser than the other 2.

CONSTANT DEMAND FOR MANPOWER

From the findings from the 3 industry players, it can be seen that the Security industry is constantly in demand of manpower. This is due to the environmental demand for security to safeguard their properties, for capabilities such as traffic control, crow control, ushering, guarding, and watchmen duties etc. This is also mainly due to the perceived low status, low salary, and the long hours that many will shun. The industry is not able to retain many young people and often gets the elderly or retired to work. The turnover rate is generally quite high and job satisfaction is low. The requirement of part time officers to act as buffer and relief are constant, and young people who joined part time events security comes and goes, moves about to various companies, therefore there is always a fighting need from security agencies to attract the limited number of people from the same pool together. But in general sense, there is always a need for someone to look after the life and property and make sure things are in order.

TIGHTENING OF SECURITY STANDARD BY THE REGULATORY

With the WDA launching of compulsory courses and the Police Licensing Regulatory Division tightening of standard by imposing the required course to be taken, 2 out of the 3 industry players agrees that the tightening of standard has helped to improve the standards of the security personnel as compared to more than a decade back. This is to prepare all officers for the worst case scenarios and to manage incidents better, and there should never be complacency in handling security issues. However, no matter how much the tightening has been implemented, there are always rooms for improvement. The tightening helps to reflect better professionalism of the people doing the job.

CAREER CONSIDERATION FROM YOUNG SINGAPOREANS

As the job generally provides low productivity, low pay, and low satisfaction, 1 of the 3 industry players strongly agreed that local young Singaporeans will not consider a career in the security industry, due to the high level of living in Singapore. It is safer to choose the better paying jobs over the lower end ones. Moreover, there is added physical risk to the security role. However, it is undeniable that there are people who choose this path but they are in the minority. The lack of status is another factor. Younger people do not like to be looked by fellow peers when it comes to career choices.

The 2nd of the 3 industry players mentioned that young Singaporeans will still consider a career in the Security industry, but to a certain extent. This applies to the consideration for armed security such as the Auxiliary Police Force. There is certain salary and progression in certain specialized sector within the force that could still entice young people, therefore young Singaporeans may still consider joining, especially those who had been with the Police Force.

The last industry player said that young Singaporeans will consider the job, but on a part time and short term basis, as it is deemed as easy money for events work. Some were unable to find a good job and some were formerly from various uniform groups, therefore there is no need to be trained. Arguably, there is a conflict of thoughts among the 3 industry players. It has been defined that young local Singaporeans with at least a Diploma and above will likely choose a better paying and better productivity jobs over Security, unless it is an armed security role. But even then, the armed security force appeals to many Chinese and Indians from Malaysia. However, part time unarmed security appeals to young personnel who wants quicker buck and lesser responsibility, as most films pays them on a weekly basis, and there is no need for IPPT or Firearms to be carried. Moreover, these are not a permanent role to be, in the mindsets of young local Singaporeans.

According to the 3 industry players, the main factors perceived by the young local Singaporeans are the low pay, low status, and uncertainty of where it will lead one's career to. They agreed that generally, there is no progress, and getting stagnated will be the consideration for deterrence to consider the career. The job will also have certain risk and stress factor due to the nature, and the pay is low, mostly working hours is long and tedious.

The 3 industry players also stated that progression in rank and responsibility, better pay and dignity, and lastly, shorter working hours will help increase consideration for the job.

SECURITY MANAGEMENT

The 3 industry players concurred that each security films in Singapore should have at least a couple of people who are highly experience/trained in the management of business and accounting, so that they can help the overall enhancement of the security business. The experience of these people may better help to sustain and improve business according to the economy. That would be preferred by more often than not. But in general, smaller films run on lower budget and competition can be cut throat. In the industry players' opinions, they agreed that with a better remuneration package, shorter working hours, stronger management, branding, and prestige built over the security films, it can help to enhance a security business. In financial sense, strong knowledge of costing is also an added advantage to weigh between charging the fee to the clients and to pay the security personnel a worthy package to entice them, and to retain their loyalty. This is for the sake of stability and recognition of the company and its manpower alike, and the very main reasons that people do not choose to be a security personnel reasons at the very first place without those mentioned above.

ANALYSIS OF THE SECURITY SURVEY

This part will analyze the findings of surveys drawing from a combination of data generated, empirical study, and personal industry experience:

ANALYSIS OF THE PUBLIC MINDSET AND PERCEPTIONS ON THE INDUSTRY

From the finding, it can be seen that the salary of the security officer/guard is the most dislike among the civilians, where their basic salary ranged from $900 to $1100 (subject to changes) in the current market. However, the highest range is still not attractive enough, amid the price to pay comes with an average of 10 to 12 hours shift and between 4 to 6 times of rest per month. Only certain level like security supervisor and above with substantial experience allows one to secure an average gross salary of $2500 and above. In terms of job status, more than half of the sampling had felt towards the negative end. It would mean that if they have a choice, they would not do so. Although security by nature is imperative, the job scopes itself, as perceived from most, are less productive and sometimes unproductive. In terms of embarrassment, as Singaporeans understand that no job is to be looked down upon, 'embarrassment' is not the term to describe, as every job has its' own merit. Given a choice of being more qualified than to do the security job, Singaporeans will not do so. Given the impression that it is low skilled, there is a good mixture of views. Not many Singaporeans felt that it is low skilled, as potential personnel have to be certified with the WDA courses in order to be licensed, sometimes even with first aid and crowd & traffic control capabilities, to be able to execute the required tasks.

Ironically, when asked on <u>playing the standing role of security personnel</u>, more than half of the people do not absolutely feel the job as redundant. Asked on whether they felt it as being unproductive when doing stand up job, ironically again, more than half also did not agree on it. In terms of feeling low skilled in nature upon asking the people to play the standing role themselves, a good mix of responses were made, however, most goes with agree. The peculiarity of the results denotes that given by a first impression by civilians, they would not want to deem security job as low skilled, however, if to make them do the job, they would feel that the job by nature is low skilled. However, when asked to do the job, they do not fully felt that the job is redundant and unproductive, as compared to the first asked impression. Given the peculiarity of the responses, the ultimate conclusion still comes straight to the point; Singaporeans will not consider a job as a security officer/guard if they have been proven to be more qualified than the role being offered. They also felt generally that it is for the senior aged, retired personnel, and those who wish to relax more on the job.

ANALYSIS OF THE DEMAINS OF SECURITY PROFESSIONALS IN SINGAPORE

Most people felt that the security business is sustainable; this is due to the on-going needs of people to protect lives and property, and with imminent threats that are happening around the world, Singapore remains a vital target for terrorists. The first line of defense is the basic security guarding, as they make up the 'eyes' to deterrence.

While there is always room for improvement, many felt that the security industry has the potential opportunity for improvement and growth, given the right grooming and strategy of strong business acumen. In all, almost all participants would agree that Singapore will consistently need a good number of security manpower to safeguard all residential and commercials buildings alike. With all, it also depends on the macro factor, such as the global trends. If the global threat is prominent and pervasive, the need to boost up security at this period is imperative. And we see that the capabilities have to be strengthened and enhanced following the global situation.

ANALYSIS OF SELF-DEFENCE SKILLS FOR SECURITY PERSONNEL

In the participating conclusion, almost all civilians felt that all security personnel, namely, even just a guard or officer, should be enhanced with the capability of self-defence skills. Only a minority had agreed with the licensing regulatory that security personnel need no training on that. In terms of which art of self-defence best suits a security personnel's capability, most would deem Israeli Military Force Self-defence suits best, as it was born in Israel for their military force, while the 2nd choice goes with the MMA (mixed martial arts), which consist of a range of martial arts combined with ground work and hand combat. The last goes with Wing Chun, a martial art of Bruce Lee's origin derived from a lady monk who had created this form of self-defence which was widely promoted by the popular grandmaster 'Ip Man'. In the survey, only martial arts have been stated as choices for participants to choose from, rather than the defensive tactics, as the martial arts are more traditional and readily recognized by the public as compared to defensive tactics available for the Forces. But in the analysis of cultural dimensions of Singapore, the second choice of self-defence, the mixed martial arts would be a selected choice, because many local Singaporeans of difference races can do MMA (mixed martial arts), as they do not appeal to only a certain group of races.

TIGHTENING OF SECURITY STANDARD

The tightening of security standard does help potential security personnel to gain a higher recognition and training proficiency, however, this does not fully appeal to young people with Diploma and above standard. This seems to only help the lower educated middle aged to feel better in terms of their dignity and pride to attaining the certificate in their course of study.

USING CRONBACH'S ALPHA

In my specialist course of applied learning and teaching, I have learnt that the Cronbach's Alpha system is a coefficient system of reliability that is commonly used for measurements of internal consistency for test scores. It is widely used by academics nowadays. It is also useful to measure the consistency of the results across some of the questions being administered for a test or survey. For example, perceived opportunity for growth consists of 3 questions in the survey that are similar and designed to measure the same factor. By leveraging on Cronbach's alpha, one can test the internal consistency of all 3 questions. Another example will be, if a survey participant were to answer 'agree' in the first 1 question, 'strongly disagree' in the second question, and then 'strongly agree' in the subsequent questions, this may result in low internal rate of consistency score. Cronbach is a common statistical tool for social science, psychology, business, and widely use by Academics and Educator alike. However, in most organizations or institutions, a benchmark of 0.7 percent and above will deemed to be the ideal score for consistency while 1.0 stands for 100% consistent. The following table consists of the Cronbach's Alpha of the samples collected:

Construct	Cronbach's Alpha	Items (Questions used in Survey)
Mindset of the people	0.895	Question 5, 6, 7
Business Opportunity perceived	0.813	Question 2, 3, 4
Perceived self-defence skills	0.85	Questions 8, 9, 10,

for personnel to be trained		11
General perception of job	0.915	Question 1
Industry Growth perceived	0.735	Question 12

The criterion rating for the Cronbach's alpha internal rate of consistency:

Cronbach's Alpha	Internal Rate of Consistency
a = 1.0	Perfect
a> / = .9	Excellent
a> / = .8	Good
a> / = .7	Acceptable
a> / = .6	Questionable
a> / = .5	Poor
a < 0.5	Unacceptable

Almost all of the 5 construct have at least an acceptable level and above. According to the criterion rating table, industry growth perceived is the lowest among the consistency rate, as the participants are the general public, therefore may have a mixed perception of the industry for growth. According to the research rating by a researcher Nunnally in 1970s, a 0.7 and above is as per mentioned, acceptable for a research, while a slightly lower rating of 0.6 are acceptable for exploratory research.

REVIEW OF THE OVERALL ANALYSIS

Overall, from the analysis given above, it can be seen that most of the potential security personnel would likely be 30 years of age and above, with an education level of below diploma. People, who are below the age of 30, but with a level below diploma, may still choose other options such as retail or sales over security guarding, as they are young. Given that, we still do not rule out the possibility of people below the age of 30, and below the level of diploma joining the security industry. This is visually common, especially for those working as reliefs. With people who are above 30, but below the level of diploma, doing security will be an option to them. With most of all who are above 30 of age, and have an education level of Diploma and above, security jobs seems to be a 'no go' to them. However, there is still a minority with Diploma and above, who chooses to be in the security industry. An average of 10 to 12 hours per shift of work, and 1 day per week rest does not appeal to most people who could choose not to. The security industry is sustainable, despite the on-going terrorism around the world. It is imperative in most case. There cannot have nobody to act as a form of deterrence, therefore the demand is always there. In terms of growth, depending on how much the security demand is necessary depends on the demographic, and the risk level raised by the Intel. If the global threat has announced attacks that are imminent to the proximity of Singapore, the risk level zone will be raised to higher, and the government military and the security guarding force will increase their guarding strength, coupled with the need for more man power and eyes to join the security industry to boost up the government military and security armed forces.

OVERVIEW SUMMARY

The chapter has covered all the research's data and information collated. It encompassed the masked profiles of respondents, analysis of research findings for both in-depth interview and surveys, and the consistency rate of individual questions using 'cronbach alpha'. The discussions can help researcher(s) to better understand the mindset of specific group of people in considering a role in the security, to confirm the sustainability of the industry, and to determine the growth of the industry. The finding and analysis has been generated to answer the questions of the research objectives, and to formulate recommendations for implementation to the research. The original surveys and interview questions will be reflected in this book as annexes or appendices just for reference. The main goal of this book is just for the readers' personal reading pleasure and the understanding of the industry in Singapore.

CHAPTER EIGHT

CONCLUSION AND RECOMMENDATION

INTRODUCTION

This is the last chapter that concludes the whole research. It will discuss the implication based on the four objectives, and implementations of the research's finding and analysis. The research objectives will be addressed and the recommendations can be put forth to companies. The limitation and future direction of the research will be described. The study will wrap up with its conclusion. Lastly, some bonus essential will be included for self-protection and security.

IMPLICATION

The research's implication will be concluded based on the four objectives of the research:

Objective 1: To evaluate the opportunity for growth in the Security Industry in Singapore.

Since 9-11, terrorism has been popularized and is pervasive over the globe. In Singapore, security is always imperative. It is an essential part of daily living in the commercial and residential industries. The growth of the Business in the Industry depends on the need of the government forces and private sectors alike, and most importantly, the frequency of terrorist attacks revolving around the globe. Unless there are more terrorists attacks around the world which most probably the attacks will indirectly affect the situations in the Asia Pacific, the opportunity for growth will remain slow but steady. Strategically, the opportunity for growth depends very much on the threats level analyzed by the local intelligence which sees the need for security to be heightened and that more manpower will be needed to protect lives and properties.

Ultimately, the growth in the Security business will be imminent. This is due to the threats of ISIS that is now generating a major amount of influence around the world. The current business of the biggest Security player remains in good hand, while with the stricter regulations and audit checks by the police licensing division to increase the standard of security firms and security personnel alike, smaller films who could not make the cut gets slashed from the industry. In all, the 2 biggest players, Certis Ciscos and Aetos Security have made the biggest revenues by offering more capabilities and hiring schemes suitable for people who are higher qualified. The joining bonus was then up to $10 000 just a couple of years ago, which means that the 2 biggest players were making big time revenues and is still doing so, even with the cut of the joining bonus. The growth of the 2 biggest industry players may also be due to the slashing of smaller rookie players, which many security personnel will tend to join the better players in Singapore in the hope of bigger earning income and benefits. The smaller players with 'A grading' also generally appeals to security personnel to join them. With better management of security films, which attracts good grading, it will attracts more security personnel to join them.

Lastly, stronger managers and directors may be able to help re-structure the business and oversees the overall hierarchy of organization. Using people from the direct industry to manage may not be as efficient in terms of strategy. On one hand, in terms of operation wise and the ability to understand the plight of ground level staffs, the middle managers of the operations would be in the better position to do so, while those in the higher level with thought leadership and strategic planning, who may be exposed to other form of businesses and has higher attainment in the business may be better to oversee the standard and procedure of the security business. Yet, the higher level managers like the general managers and chief officers must also walk the ground to learn the root of the ground and talk to the ground level staffs in order to contribute well to the overall higher attainment in business and management.

Objective 2: To understand a person's preference and mindset in considering a security career.

The overall perception of young people (30 years and below) with a qualification of Diploma and above are that they could have done something more challenging, better pay, better fulfillment, better productivity, non-uniformed, and higher dignity, as compared to something mundane, lower pay, lower skilled, lower productivity, and lower dignity. Those with a qualification lower than diploma felt that Security job may be an option to a certain extent. They could have preferred armed security, which give them a slightly higher prestige, responsibility and pay, as compared to a Security guard/officer. However, we do not rule out that there are also many, who prefer to be a security guard/officer, and choose not to hold the responsibility of carrying a firearm. A person (60 of age and above) who has a qualification lesser than a diploma, and is on retirement to sustain himself/herself, would tend to take on a Security role, amid other possible job of their former specializations, such as technician, fork lift driver, van driver, or even taxi driver. In terms of pride, younger people would also not want the public or their peers to see them standing guard in uniform in the public or seating around shopping malls or condominiums, which does not sync with their pride and mindset, therefore this is not a career to them, especially in Singapore.

Objective 3: To analyze the demand of security professionals to be hired in Singapore, in lieu of prevalent terrorism around the world.

The demand for security professionals are always there and this research has categorized them into both positive and negative demands.

Negative demands: High Turnover, for the armed and unarmed security industry, therefore the need for more manpower is always there. The long working hours in general and the subjective changes of the Human Resource benefits and policy in some companies is also one of the factors citing the turnover. Part time unarmed officers are constantly in demand due to ad-hoc events such as festival seasons and major national events. The part time officers comes from a diverse groups of students, retirees, and freelancers, and therefore the turnover rate has been constant due either students furthering their studies, going national services (for guys), and the biggest contributing factor would be that freelance personnel hopping around companies to join various good paying ad-hoc events etc.

Positive demands: With more demand from the government forces and residential areas to secure their buildings for deterrence, watcheyes, protecting lives and properties, the need for manpower has expanded and thus new people are needed to join the industry. On top of security capabilities such as crowd control, traffic control, bank guarding, out-riding, security guarding, protection service, private investigation, and access control, the demand of other more specialized outsourcing capabilities which range from armed shooting range for MINDEF to fitness instruction for IPPT, the security players had also set up trainings to recruit and train these niche of people to join them, therefore the demand expands.

Objective 4: To study whether the tightening of standard by the Police Licensing Regulatory Department has improved the standard of the security professionals to effectively handle security and counter-terrorism situation.

The tightening of standard by the Police Licensing Regulatory Department has to a good extent, improved the standard of security personnel. For example, the course on crowd control and handle counter terrorism helps them to better be aware and handle situations more efficiently. The certification does increase their dignity and morale in some ways, and act as a form of development, which become the best of both worlds.

Over the decade, the average 12 hourly shift rates have grown from $40 per day to $80 per day, with some assignments even higher rate. The continuous requirement for certain certifications has helped the group of officers to constantly upgrade and stay relevant to the industry, following the wage model. The photo licensing also helps them to be identified as security personnel, which gives them an overall better identity and verification. For this pool of officers, they are 'better' now as compared to a decade before. However, more could always be done. To drastically do more, crisis and risk will have to be prevalent in the country itself. As compared to the states, the security risk is in Singapore is very much lower, especially with the 'no-firearms' law in Singapore. With overall low security risk in Singapore, the need to create high end VIP protection security personnel in the private security industry is close to none, except that the government police force has an elite team of Security Command officers (body guard), who are supposed to be with their principal (the government VVIPs) 24 hours a day, which their sleep hours are on standby.

Although the government forces has standby a few teams of elite tactical units to physically deal with riots and terrorism, the private security business is still ruled by the government regulatory, therefore a lot of constraint and regulations are there, which the businesses could not expand capability and build a team of high end armed security personnel. The strongest reason would be the lack of demand in Singapore that creates a control by the government regulatory.

BASIC RECOMMENDATION

For the Auxiliary Police Force: Generate a rank and pay system for the auxiliary police force that is close to the uniformed state police officers. The color of the uniform should revert to darker blue, as compared to the current steel or greenish blue, and the combat style attire should have military movement capability cargo pockets. Screening process should also be more stringent, in response to cases of auxiliary police officers themselves committing crimes (during off duties) and suicide (during duties). Psychometric tests and psychologically assessment should be conducted for them.

For unarmed security forces: Age limit of officers up to age 80 to cut off. For those who are 80 and above and still wishes to work, they must be certified 'fit to work' by the local doctor, and go through a thorough assessment checklist on their motivation to work. All other ages follows the pre-employment check up regulation as usual. The uniforms should also be standardized across the nation to increase pride and motivation. For example, combat style could be introduced for standing security officers to create a tougher and more macho appearance. Taking the examples of security officers from Indonesia, it could be seen that the men in blue seems to be physically ready for any situation. Older security officers above the age of 65 may be given an option to wear non-combat uniform, but all protection equipments must be carried. Weapons, such night stick should be implemented across all unarmed personnel for self-protection purposes, as the guards are deemed to be the first respondents to situations within their parameter. Basic self-defence and unarmed tactics should be introduced, on top of their certifications to be taken. In most of the situation, terrorists initial planned take down will be the security personnel, to prevent them from reporting or alarming the rest of the people, before an attack continues.

Recommended range of basic pay-scale: For Auxiliary Police Officers, $1500 to $1700 (For N level holders and above), and $1800 to $2000 (For diploma/degree holders). For unarmed security, basic pay-scale ranged from $1100 (For secondary 2) to $1600 (for diploma holders). These salaries are not inclusive of other risk allowances, overtimes, and AWS etc.

Minimum rank system for the Auxiliary Police Officers should be 'Lance corporal' and above, as compared to previous 'constable'. This is to help increase the rank system to a level higher, yet, not on par with the rank system of the state police, as per regulated previously. The security officer can remain status quo of starting from a rank of 'protection specialist' or 'security officers' up to a rank of Executive Protection Specialists and Chief Security Officer respectively, however, a duration of the rank progression must be made transparently and openly to all individuals, in order to set a direction for the individual for their career goals. This rank progression during can match closely to the new Progressive wage model.

Increasing operation capability such as overseas escorts and personal protections can be an added prestige to be offered by top notch security films. However, regardless of armed or unarmed personnel, self-defence and unarmed tactics must be trained to the individual personnel to diffuse situations and response to the first hand scenario, while awaiting the police's arrival. Watching to report and guarding to deter does not always work against highly trained insurgents or aggressors, therefore a security officers must not only be competent in knowledge of security operations, but also in physical as well.

In management, smaller companies could do a strategic analysis of other successful companies of other industries to learn their success formula, in order to increase their own competency. The second common ingredient for management stuffs is to attend corporate trainings and workshops that is relevant to their management training needs for the organizations, to enhance their capability. Taking a business diploma, degree or higher degree in business may also help the management level staffs see things in a broader perspective and able to generate new innovations and ideas for problem solving and implementations of the organization. Security films needs more high level management staffs that are brilliant and/or have high level of business management acumen to address all problems in a more competent and professional manner. Most of all, the pay scale must be met for potential high level management staffs whom the organization has faith to hire. This serves to help security film to come to a higher level overall.

LIMITATION OF THE RESEARCH

Everything has its limit. Even the best one has them, not to say for this piece of study. Firstly, this is due to the research has been done in a span of just few weeks to conduct the surveys and the in-depth interviews, on top of working full time. The sample size of the survey is significantly small, as compared with the 5.5 million of people in Singapore. The significantly small number of respondents may somehow, affect the research outcome, as well as the reliability. Fortunately, it can still be seen that the samplings in this study are reliable.

Additionally, though all the survey and in-depth interview questionnaires were completed under my supervision as the researcher, the participated civilian's different personality and values are still the potential attribution to the research, which may affect the choice they made. Besides, this is the 2nd time I have conducted the interviews and surveys. Hence the limited experience and skills may also somehow affect both the qualitative and quantitative study in some ways. Fortunately, I have some prior knowledge of research, which helps to scaffold the research process. But as always, more improvements could be made with better teaching and guidance from my previous research supervisor.

FUTURE DIRECTION OF RESEARCH, AND CONCLUSION

This research mainly encompasses the 4 objectives. There is no overt hypothesis in this paper; however, the research objectives are being addressed to create a stronger and deeper understanding of the current trends and situations, and the finding of the mindsets of Singaporeans. To some extent, the overhaul of the security industry that is relevant to the business, and the imperative needs for security to be heightened, denotes the need for more manpower, which the growth is viable, but not all drastic yet. Hence with that, the future studies will revolves the global and strategic studies, which may significantly impact the demand of the security business and its' industry.

On one hand, if the global situation ever allows the demand for more elite high end security to be created, it would mean a likelihood that former members of the elite in the army and police will join, as well as more highly educated personnel, coupled with military, fitness, fighting spirits, and martial arts background would be interested. This has happened in U.S where there are a lot of Army/Police veterans who had joined as private military/security contractors with a renowned Private Military/Security company such as 'Blackwater Ops'. On the other hand, it this had to be formed in Singapore, it would mean that Singapore is at an all high level risk of threats, where gun laws had to be changed, should there ever be a need for our nation to demand such a creation of these gung-ho elites. With these, the future research will study the terrorism trends around the world and the situations revolving around the neighbouring countries. The potential fifth wave of terrorism can also be placed into consideration for study and investigation, together with the global terrorism trends and situations revolving around the neighbouring countries, as mentioned just earlier.

END OF SECURITY INDUSTRY RESEARCH

CHAPTER NINE

BASIC SECURITY ESSENTIALS

INTRODUCTION

This chapter introduces some of the basic security essentials one can have, in order to be a person with a better overall sense of security and protection for himself/herself. Unlike the previous chapters which discussed the research on the security industry in a more formal manner, this chapter is a bonus chapter which will describe the basic essentials of protecting oneself, in a more personal context, direct to readers. However in doing so, I disclaim any liability for accidents or injuries that may arise as a result of the information given in this chapter, which is only intended as a work of advice. Of course, effort has been made to ensure that the information given is correct at the time of writing. However, some of the information given may by its nature, anecdotal, changeable or disputable, there it cannot be assumed to be authoritative, universal or exhaustive.

1. KEEPING FIT

Keeping fit in general helps in situation such as the need to run from an assailant with a knife, during gang fights (which you may not be involved but as an innocent victim to be), active shootings (in countries with authorized arm carry laws), or any situations that create frantic moment to escape from the location. Keeping fit may not be easy for some due to age, weight, and diseases, but the better ability to move around, run, climb, crawl or hide helps to make good difference. Keeping fit allows one to have a better mental alertness, confidence, and speed of reaction during the time of need. So, just do your best to keep fit by exercising or working out whenever you can, or at least go for a slow jog. The gist of saying 'to keep fit' at the very core of my first meaning is to ask you to be able to run. If you can run faster than your assailant in times of frantic situation, you will most likely be able to escape serious injury or even death. Of course, if you are being cornered, you will have to turn and push through your way out like a spear, coupled with adrenalin and the will to live. But do not be surprised to suffer absorption of damages. At least you will have more than 50% chance of survival.

2. SITUATIONAL AWARENESS

Our local government encourages the community to be vigilant and report any irregularities to the authority. This is 'Situational Awareness'. Being able to take note of the surrounding and feel the situation around you helps you to be more alert and able to mentally prepare you for threatening situation that you may be able to mitigate. Having situational awareness can make you less vulnerable and response better to any crisis. However, it is undeniable that the advent of gadgets such as mobile phones and tablets has made us so absorbed into the devices that our situational awareness ability seems to fade. Fret not, with more discipline, control and moderation of usage of devices when on the moves, the ability of situational awareness that you need, will return.

3. UNPREDICTABILITY

Being unpredictable helps you to be able to prevent any surveillance against you. In local context, potential robbery, theft, and stalking may aim towards you or your property. Do simple unpredictable moves like going on a different routes to work every day. Car can be parked at different lots and different timing within the same precinct. And if your work time is staggered, do not need to reveal to your neighbours. Create a sense of mystery and confusion to people in your neighbourhood who may be watching you for any reasons. Be it just a harmless busybody neighbour, or a real potential threat to be committed against you, creating a sense of mystery and confusion to them may either deter, if not, mitigate the threats.

4. SELF-DEFENCE SKILLS

Having Martial Art skills is useful as it equips you for a lifetime (provided you remember all the moves). But with enough practice or as a regular practitioner, the skills you learn may ingrain into your bloodstream and the moves and reflexes stays with you in times of need. However, if you did not practice any martial arts in your life time, you could still go for self-defence workshops such as Israeli Krav Maga, Russian Martial Arts Systema, or some hybrid arts created by some experts around the globe. Learn them by heart, or remember as much as you can. Otherwise, do consider the more conventional martial arts commonly found in Community Centres/Clubs or Associations such as Karate, Silat, Taekwondo, Muay Thai, Tai Chi, or Kickboxing. There are other more sophistical self-defence workshops like applying the use of 'Torchlights' in self-defence, 'Kerambit (special shaped knife)', and 'Kobutan (Pen light sharp object), which may be conducted by instructors versed in Silat and Philipino martial arts (Eg 'Kali (stick) weapon' or 'Escrimas') etc. Having Martial Art skills or self-defence skills makes you a harder target more often than you are not. But remember the hard truth; nothing is 100% effective in defence against an attack, especially with an assailant holding a knife or gun. There are many different techniques of defending against a knife assailant. Go for 1 of the workshops, and analyze to see its effectiveness. For gun defence, it is usually simulated at close range. In real active shoot out, it would be a distance kill. What most workshop teaches are guns being pointed at close range. The problem would be, a close range gun point would likely meant that the assailant is not intending to kill you whole heartedly at the first place, or it could just be an attempted robbery, or hostage situation. It the gun holder is out to kill you whole heartedly, he would most likely fire at you from a distance that you may not have the much time to react. In general, do not go for too many workshops, as the techniques may confuse you, especially when you are a season martial artist.

5. IMPROVISED SELF–DEFENCE TOOLS

There are various defensive tools in your life that are commonly seen and usable. Some of the items you can think of are; umbrella, pen, torchlight, walking sticks, spray (insecticides), selfie-sticks, helmets, bags, keys, chairs and any items deemed as hard. The tools, for example, pen helps you to neutralize a low risk assailant by stabbing onto his thigh. Of course, the more extreme counter-offence example is to stab into the assailants' eye blinding him/her. But please do not do that, unless you are in the desperate moment of your own life and death.

Chairs can be used as shields against assailants with sticks and long knives. It can also be used to fling against assailants before escaping.

Long items, example an umbrella and walking stick requires a little application of techniques from martial arts to control and retrain an assailant.

Bags can be used as cover against sticks and knives attack (though it could not protect one totally).

Helmets are hard, and can be used as shields against long/short knives (parang) attack if apply properly with some focus. It can also be used as a counter-offensive tool to hit back an assailant with long/short knife. So for those who are riding, you can be quite safe against assailants.

6. FIRE ARMS

In Singapore, all guys are conscripted into the Army, Police, or SCDF for their national services. Basically, for most guys who are combat fit, they would have gone through some form of firearms training in their life time. At least rifles like M-16 or SAR-21 has been the conscripted men's 'wives' during their tenure, while those in the police would have learnt a revolver as their 'babies'. With the strict 'no guns' law here, the advantageous point would be that in any form of dangerous situation be it ever in Singapore or in an overseas country with guns around, getting the hands on the guns proves better for Singaporean guys as compared to those guys from other countries who have not touched the guns in their life time. The chances of getting defensive upon able to hold on to a gun and fire back at an assailant would give a greater edge of survivability than those not trained in any forms of firearms. This is fortunate that most Singaporean men are combat ready. Now the only thing will be left for, are the ladies. Guns like Singapore Rifle Associations and Singapore Gun Club are good ground for orientating on the use of hand guns or shot guns. Get familiarize with handguns such as Glock, Beretta, or SigPro so that in any situation and you have a chance to use it, use it. As for rifles, the most basic a woman can get used to in the rifle range there, would be the modified M-16 with smaller calibers compared to the real deal. For shot guns, it would come under the property of the Singapore Gun Club. Usually the deal would be, a short 3 month term membership, and to shoot at a pigeon clay, simulating hunting on the birds. Learn a few firearms. Get interested in it. Make yourself more suave, and make yourself a harder target.

7. CAR SAVING TOOLS AND SAFETY

Car accidents are not uncommon. There are times that drivers will face accident due to various reasons. They could be with illnesses such as heart attack, drunk driving, being hit by other cars, suddenly burst of fire on the car front bonnet or whatever reasons one can think of. If you hit a tree and managed to survive with consciousness but the whole car is jammed with you being stuck at your driver's seat, you need a tactical tool that is possible to smash off the car windows to escape. The tool should be able to cut off your seat belt and act as a glass smasher, in order for you to be able to escape from the car window or facilitate rescuers. While you smash off your window and escape soundly, remember, a portable fire extinguisher is useful to put out the fire should your car front ever burst fire. The portable fire extinguisher should be ideally placed somewhere within your reach.

Others essentials items should include long torchlight (best your forearm length), which is useful for item searches within the car should the car interior be dark or when the car lights are deemed insufficient. The long torchlight would also act as a handy self-defence tool in times of need. Such as to strike back at an assailant, or striking against an assailant's hand who has a knife etc.

The other useful self-defence tools like a baseball bat or umbrellas can be placed at your car side. Generally, in less hostile prone countries, it would be more practical to place umbrellas at your car side, while long torchlight can be placed close to, or squeeze through somewhere between the seats and gear box side.

Items like a portable car tyre pump and portable car battery charger would be useful if one is travelling in a country with long road distance. Items like snacks and water for drinking will be good to be placed in car, for any emergency consumption. At least a spare bottle of water for re-filling the car filter and coolant should also be kept in boots for use in times of need. The last item would be a portable mobile charger, to be kept in the car for back up purpose. Check the portable mobile charger weekly to ensure it has the store value. The charger would help to charge up your phone should there be a need to use your phone during frantic moment when your phone battery is low.

Adding miscellaneous items like Panadol/Paracetamol, axe brand oil, plaster, pens, notepad, sanitizers, tissues, wet tissues and spare charging cables etc in your car help you in various aspects that you could think of.

Lastly, for general personal safety, always enter your car and lock it immediately. This is to minimize being able to be carjacked by people who may be watching you or coming to you.

For environment you deemed as common and safe, do a round of check of the car by walking a clockwise/anti-clockwise direction to look out for any irregularities of the car surface, body, and underneath. This may help spot unforeseen items such as drugs, contrabands cigarettes or even improvised explosive device being planted, or any other kinds of potential sabotage.

8. DEFENSIVE DRIVING AND RIDING

For the safety as a driver and to manage control of your vehicle against other unforeseen incidents such as other dangerous drivers/riders, take up a defensive driving course. The one day course will refresh your old driving knowledge, make you do an aptitude cum psychometric test for driving, and also physically train you how to break and maneuver your car during a high speed situation, with some knowledge that a stunt driver will need to know. If you are lucky enough, the driving centre instructor may show you how to do a drift to your car. However, in saying those, I am not referring to a stunt driving course, but literally, a defensive driving course offered by a couple of driving centres in Singapore. Their main aim is to make you a safe driver on a defensive purpose to evade dangerous situations, rather than to counter-offence. For people who are usually on the road, it is good to go for a defensive driving/riding course to equip yourself to a higher level. Who knows, you may be able to use the skills to evade drivers driven by bad guys, or do your counter-offence against those cars, as a security personnel.

9. CPR + AED

In Singapore, it is stated in one source that the number 1 killer is heart attack. Having to know CPR + AED is good for you and your family members. Imagine if one of your love on suffers a heart attack or is unconscious, rendering CPR may at save their lives, while awaiting the ambulance. It is also an essential skill to be acquired by sport coaches, security officers, life guards, teachers, doctors and nurses etc. These skills are needed to help save the casualties on the ground before the arrival of the ambulance or a paramedic. Some of the providers of the course include Singapore Red Cross Society, Saint John Ambulance, Singapore Heart Foundations and Raffles Medical group etc. Easily, the skills and steps of CPR + AED can be found online or on 'youtube' videos. But to get certified properly in order to execute it in times of need, it will be crucial to take up the 4 hours course in the approved training organizations. The license card certificate will last for 2 years.

10. THIRD LANGUAGE

In Singapore, every Singaporean child is speaking two languages. The 2 languages are: English, and your racial language. On top of them, you may have known another language of your family root which is a 'dialect', which cannot be written in words. Now I will be referring to a third language which you may wish to learn. Be it Arabic, Vietnamese, Thai, Japanese, Spanish, French, or German, learning an extra language, or at least know a few words of phrases in a third language might improve your chance of avoiding or escaping a danger in the countries you may frequent on. It may help you pick up the nuances of a situation, and allow you to seek assistance in a crisis. Do not assume that the world speaks English, though it should be a globalized language. Since language creates connection, increasing the options through knowing more languages helps.

11. BOMB THREAT MANAGEMENT

Bomb threat management? Sounds like a big word. But it is useful for all to know. Yes, though Singapore has hardly encounter any bomb threat, it should never be taken as 'no' for granted. A telephone bomb threat is quite unusual, but not unknown. Be it at the office building or even at home, do not be surprise of a bomb threat call through the telephone. You may be the one picking it up. In this incident, you should:

1) Not hang up your phone – It may still be possible for the police to trace the call if even if the caller hang up the phone.

2) Do not use mobile phone – Radio signal has the potential to detonate the bomb.

3) Do not activate the fire alarm if you are at the office building.

4) Do not touch or move any packages.

5) Write a note and pass/show it to the next person at your home or office building.

6) Pay close attention to the caller, to obtain as much information as possible.

7) Take note, and ask questions on: When will it explode, where is it right now, what does it look like, what kind of bomb is it, where did the caller place it, who is the target, the intention of planting it, the address of the caller, the name of the caller.

8) Observe the caller's accent, tone, emotional state, background noise, age and gender.

9) Write down date and time of the call

10) Call the police and submit the findings to the police.

In any bomb threat situations:

1) Check the area for unfamiliar packages or items. Do not touch the suspicious item. Try to condone the items and advise those around to move as far or at least 100 metres away from the item.

2) Take your personal/important belongings when leaving.

3) Leave doors and windows open to mitigate any blast.

4) Do not turn off lights which may impair visions and caused confusions.

12. COMMUNITY WATCH

In Singapore, soft targets such as hotels, shopping centres, commercial buildings and public areas which people will congregate together, are potential areas for suspicious activities and terror attacks. Security is usually being stepped up at those areas. However, as a community at large, one can play their part by doing some of the following:

1) If noted suspicious people loitering in and around the building, inform security personnel who may in turn inform their management and police. If need be, you can call the police.

2) If you caught a glimpse of unattended bags or parcel, alert security personnel who may in turn inform their

management and police. If need be, you can call the police.

3) Keep an eye for your colleagues, family, and friends who may exhibit suspicious behavior to deter them from radicalizing themselves or others. Example of radicalization would be displaying symbols or words to support terrorist groups, expressing interest in content that promotes extremist ideologies and violence, reading up and discussing the interest to join the extremist group, and keeping contact with extremist organizations.

In identifying a suspicious person to report, note the characteristics such as the **gender, height, race, behavior, attire and what they are carrying.**

In identifying a vehicle to report, note the characteristics such as the **brand, model, colour, registration number, and any special markings.**

In identifying a suspicious package (parcels, bags or luggage etc) which may be abandoned and to report, note the characteristics such as the **shape, size, packaging and any markings.**

13. HOME ESSENTIALS

Home security is important for you and your family. In Singapore, homes are pretty safe, however, having home essentials that can help to safeguard the safety and security of the home help in deterring crimes and hazards. So what would be good to have? Below is a list of items but not exhaustive:

1) Torchlight: Best to get a length up to your forearms. Keep at least one. It can be used for blackout and even self-defence. You can easily get those at the Army market, with sharp edges near the bezel area, which can strike on assailants when necessary. Standard torchlight can also be kept, just for blackout purposes. Small torchlight such as the length of your palm can be placed in your room in times to needs and within reach.

2) Fire blanket/Portable fire extinguisher: The items can be used in times of fire hazard. Though fire safety hazard can be prevented by the high standard and

regulation of Singapore, keep a fire blanket/portable fire extinguisher will still be useful for safeguarding purpose.

3) First aid: Items such as medicines for headache, fever, cough, stomach pain, muscle aching creams, and plasters etc are essential home first aid.

4) Security Camera: In home such as HDB, security camera may not be too necessary, unlike private properties. However, there are people who install mini surveillance camera accessible via mobile phones and laptops in their HDB homes. For those people who does not need to install the mini camera, installing a dummy camera still help in certain percentage of crime deterrence. In many houses, superstitious people install the fengshui 'Bagua' (Hexagon) mirror in front of their home to deflect evil. Having a normal round mirror placed above the door can also help you to view better in case of unwanted people stalking or following behind you, which can help you to react faster in times of necessity.

5) When leaving home, remember to lock the window grills to deter burglars, and close windows to prevent rain from wetting the home. People may also dump in cigarette butts that may cause fire hazard, or dumping rubbish out of pranks (This is also depending on the level you stay, and the location the window faces), therefore close the windows when leaving home. If you are at home, you can choose to open the windows and even the doors as you are there to monitor and react, but always lock the door grills and window grills.

6) Lastly, if you are less open to neighbours, at least know a neighbour at the unit just beside you, or at least someone from a unit within your view. This is because the neighbour and his/her family may be able to watch your home in times of needs or when travelling overseas with no one is around. They would be able to provide some observations in case of any irregularities occurred and you can take further future preventive measures. If you have newspaper being delivered to your home every day but feels a hassle to stop the delivery, offer the newspapers to be kept by the neighbour watching your home for you, so that there

will be no obvious sign for potential burglars to note your home has no one, for a period of time. Having an extra pair of watcheyes increase chance to deter any attempts of unwanted actions at your unit.

14. TACTICAL VEST

Having in the conscripted army and volunteered as a police officer, a Tactical Vest and a replica helmet would be deemed useful to have for keepsake. This is where you can buy it readily at tactical stores etc and place in your fitness plates for cross weighted training and jogging purpose. Though this may not be an amour or Kevlar vest or helmet that you may want it to be, it is better to none. It would help you in times of combat needs. Remember, Singapore has less likely chance of one becoming a hero, but if you had read about the SAS guy in Zimbabwe, you would have thought that a training vest in your car etc is useful for counter-terrorism purpose. However again, unlike certain countries, Singapore do not allow one to own a firearm, therefore having a weighted tactical vest helps you in the approach of being protected with lesser than the impact of injuries sustained on one that is without a weighted vest or helmet on.

References

Singapore steps up efforts to counter terrorism / Our News / Singapore United - Community Engagement Programme Portal. 2013. Singapore steps up efforts to counter terrorism / Our News / Singapore United - Community Engagement Programme Portal. [ONLINE] Available at: http://www.singaporeunited.sg/cep/index.php/web/Our-News/Singapore-steps-up-efforts-to-counter-terrorism. [Accessed 10 March 2013].

Stirling, R., 2009. Special Forces. London: John Blake Publishing Ltd

Singapore's Approach To Counterterrorism - War on Terrorism - Zimbio. 2013. Singapore's Approach To Counterterrorism - War on Terrorism - Zimbio. [ONLINE] Available at: http://www.zimbio.com/War+on+Terrorism/articles/kshAiUYcLK8/Singapore+Approach+Counterterrorism. [Accessed 10 March 2013].

Nadarajan, B., 2012. Close Watch. A Nation's Resolve to Secure Singapore, p.131.

Publisher 2013. . [ONLINE] Available at: http://newagepublishers.com/samplechapter/000896.pdf. [Accessed 18 March 2013].

Gagliardi, G., 2004. Strategy Against Terror. Seattle: Clearbridge.

Business 2000 Resources - Glossary - Case Studies for the Classroom. Business Case Studies, Economics Case Studies, LCVP Case Studies.. 2013. Business 2000 Resources - Glossary - Case Studies for the Classroom. Business Case Studies, Economics Case Studies, LCVP Case Studies.. [ONLINE] Available at: http://www.business2000.ie/resources/Glossary_L.html. [Accessed 12 March 2013].

Literature Reviews - The Writing Center. 2012. Literature Reviews - The Writing Center. [ONLINE] Available at: http://writingcenter.unc.edu/handouts/literature-reviews/. [Accessed 7 October 2012].

Drucker, P., 1967. The Effective Decision. Harvard Business Review on Decision Making, pp.1-19.

Security Business Opportunities. 2013. Security Business Opportunities. [ONLINE] Available at: http://www.securitybusinessopportunities.com/. [Accessed 3 March 2013].

NTUC LearningHub - WSQ Manage Security Business. 2012. NTUC LearningHub - WSQ Manage Security Business. [ONLINE] Available at: http://www.ntuclearninghub.com/manage-security-business. [Accessed 16 November 2013].

Bazerman, M., 2002. Judgment in Managerial Decision Making. United States of America: John Wiley & Sons.

Research Papers - Singapore . 2012. Research Papers - Singapore. [ONLINE] Available at: http://www.spp.nus.edu.sg/aci/Research_Output_Singapore.aspx. [Accessed 12 December 2013].

Mayer, B., 2009. Who Dares Wins. New York: Pocket Books.

Asia-Pacific Economic Cooperation. 2012. Page Not Found - Asia-Pacific Economic Cooperation. [ONLINE] Available at: http://www.apec.org/Home/Groups/SOM-Steering-Committee-on-Economic-and-Technical-Cooperation/Task-Groups/Counter-Terrorism-Task-Force. [Accessed 10 October 2012].

Here's $8,000, come join us | The New Paper. 2013. Here's $8,000, come join us | The New Paper. [ONLINE] Available at: http://www.tnp.sg/content/heres-8000-come-join-us. [Accessed 8 February 2013].

Mcnab, A., 1993. Bravo Two Zero. Britain: Bantam Press..

Counter Terrorism and Security. 2013. Counter Terrorism and Security. [ONLINE] Available at: http://www.cbsgroup.com.sg/security.asp. [Accessed 11 March 2013].

Terral, J., 2006. Seals Battlecraft. USA: The Berkley Publishing Group.

Ministry of Home Affairs - Extracts of Minister's Interview
with Zaobao. 2012. Ministry of Home Affairs - Extracts of
Minister's Interview with Zaobao. [ONLINE] Available at:
http://www.mha.gov.sg/news_details.aspx?nid=NDMz-
4huJrUrqBIc%3d. [Accessed 15 December 2012].

More women opting to work in security industry. 2013. More
women opting to work in security industry. [ONLINE]
Available at:
http://www.asiaone.com/Business/Office/Hot%2BJobs/Story/A
1Story20080102-43280.html. [Accessed 5 November 2012].

Mcnab, C., 2008. Special Forces Survival Guide. United
Kingdom: Amber Books Ltd.

MEK Munshi, M.H.A.K., 1999. Principles & Practice of
Management. Singapore: S.S Mubaruk & Brothers Pte. Ltd.

Market Research Reports - Research and Markets -
Information. 2013. Market Research Reports - Research and
Markets - Information. [ONLINE] Available at:
http://www.researchandmarkets.com/reports/29200/the_securit

y_industry_business_ratio_report. [Accessed 18 December 2012].

SIA | Home . 2013. SIA | Home. [ONLINE] Available at: http://www.siaonline.org/. [Accessed 5 January 2013].

Haney, E.L., 2002. Inside Delta Force. New Yotk: Bantam Dell.

Security Industry - International Security - United Press International - UPI.com. [ONLINE] Available at: http://www.upi.com/Business_News/Security-Industry/. [Accessed 1 March 2013].

John s. Hammond, R.L.K., 2002. Smart Choice. United States of America: Broadway Books.

Kheng-Hor, K., 1995. Applying Sun Tzu's Art of War in Corporate Politics. Malaysia: Pelanduk Publications.

WDA. 2013.. [ONLINE] Available at: http://www.wda.gov.sg/content/dam/wda/pdf/Speeches/210820 12/NDOC%20Factsheet_20120808_CMC_V02_final.pdf. [Accessed 23 March 2013].

APPENDIX

Dislike salary (in blue)
2
37%
1
63%

Dislike long working hours (In blue)
3
19%
2
9%
1
72%

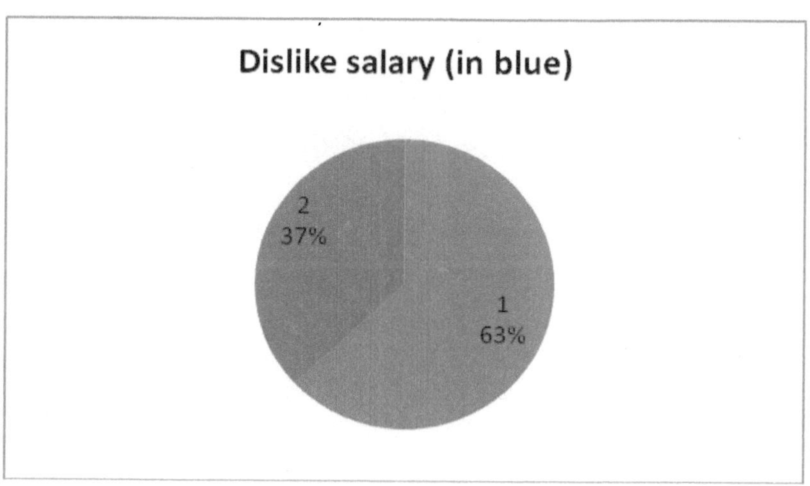

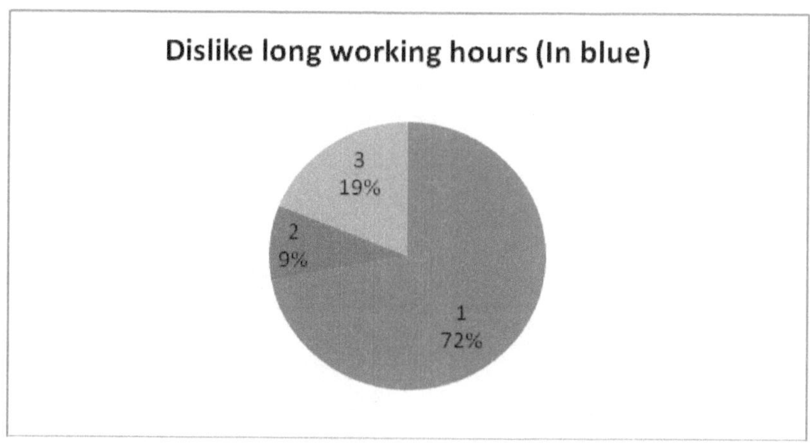

Felt neutral with Job status (In blue)
Disliek with Job status (In red)
2
45%
1
55%

APPENDIX

Unproductiveness - 64% felt unproductive, 26% felt neutral
Series1
70
60
50
40
30
20
10
0
1
2

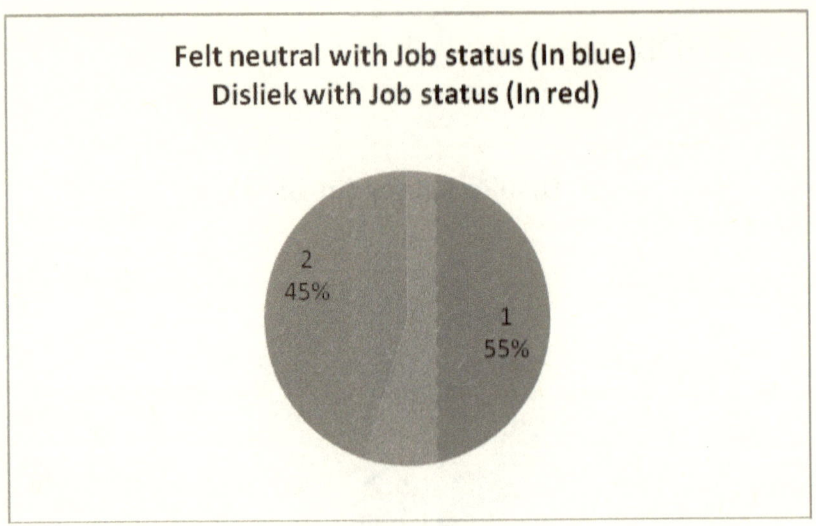

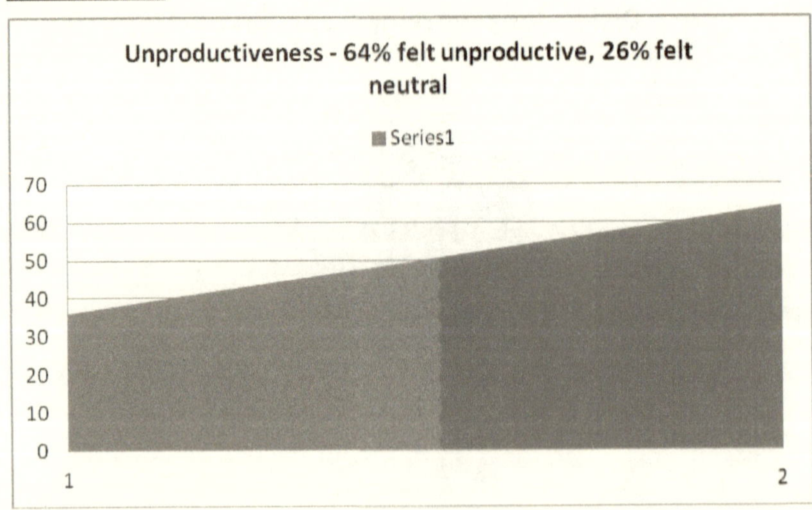

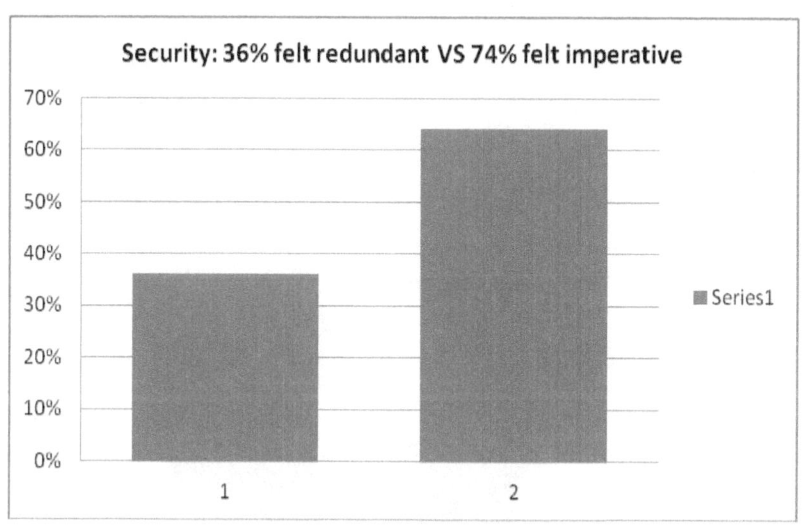

Security: 36% felt redundant VS 74% felt imperative
70%
60%
50%
40%
30%
20%
10%
0%
1
2
Series1

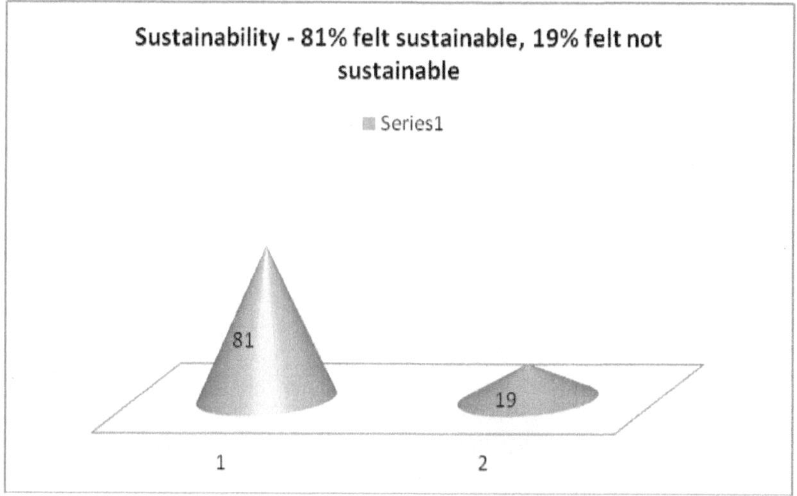

Sustainability - 81% felt sustainable, 19% felt not sustainable
Series1
81
19
1
2

APPENDIX

Potential opportunity to grow
Agree
27%
73%

91% agree security needs a good number of manpower, while 9% disagree
2
9
1
91

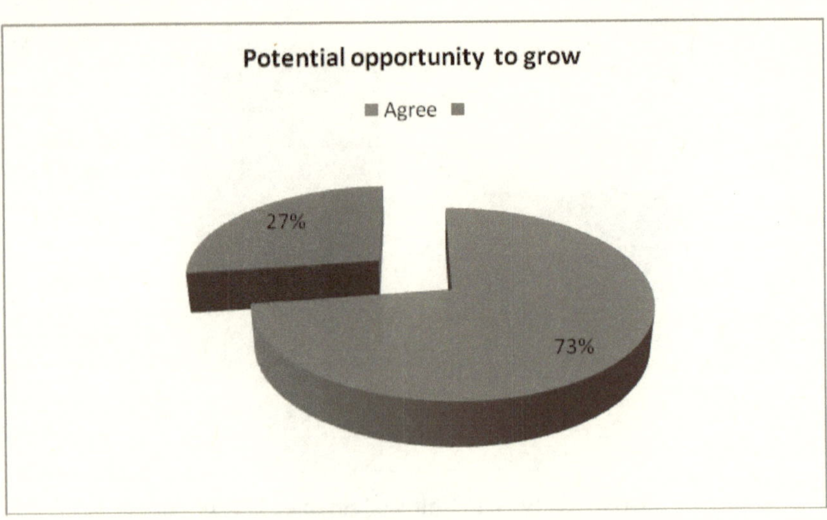

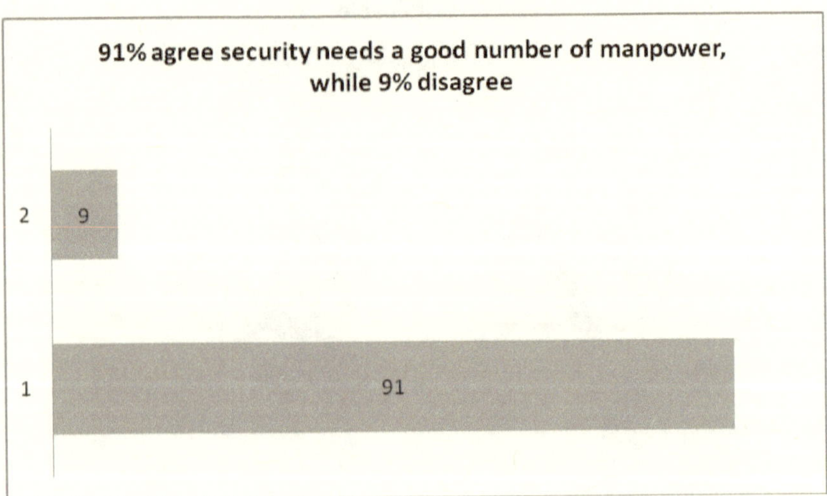

Opportunity for growth despite the outsourcing needs -
73% agree to strongly agree, 9% neutral, 19% disagree
80
70
60
50
40
30
20
10
0
1
2
3

<u>APPENDIX</u>

Enhancing capability - 82% agree to strongly
agree, 18% disagree to strongly disagree
2
18%
1
82%

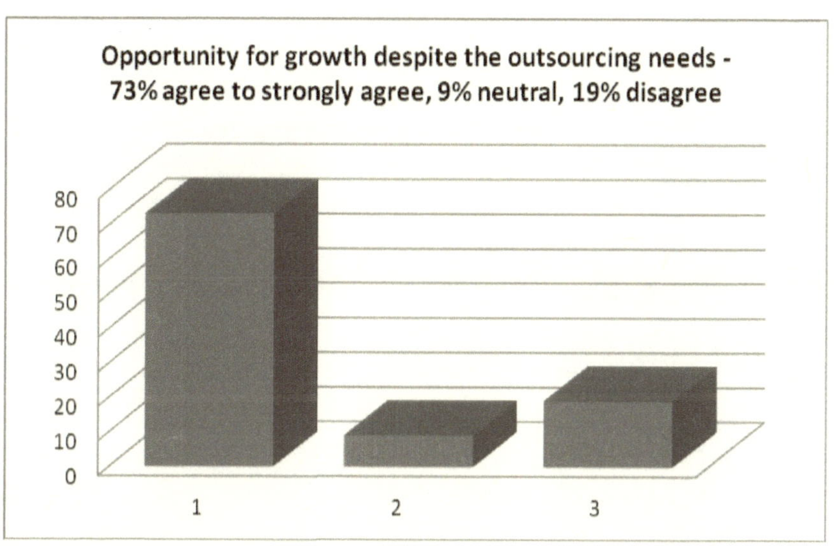

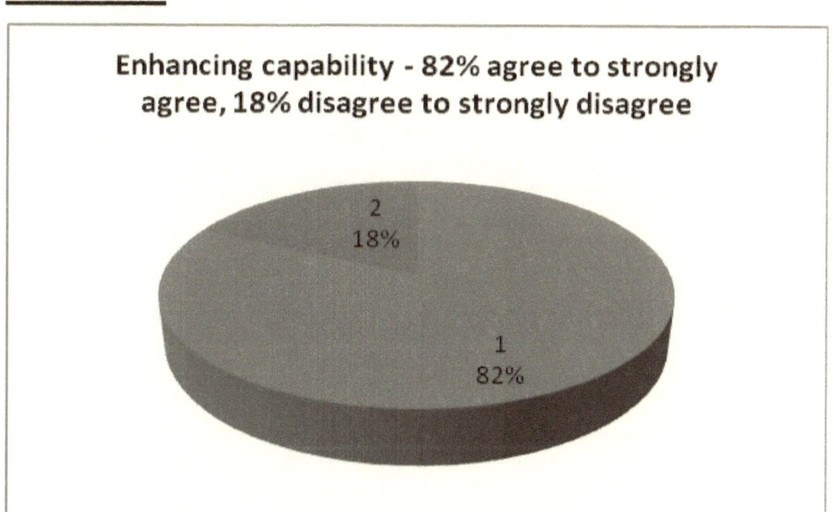

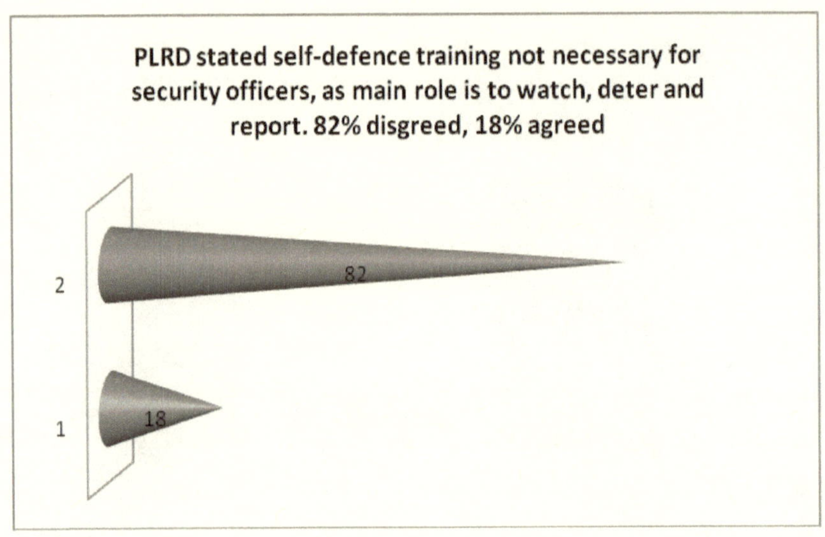

PLRD stated self-defence training not necessary for security officers, as main role is to watch, deter and report. 82% disgreed, 18% agreed
2
82
1
18

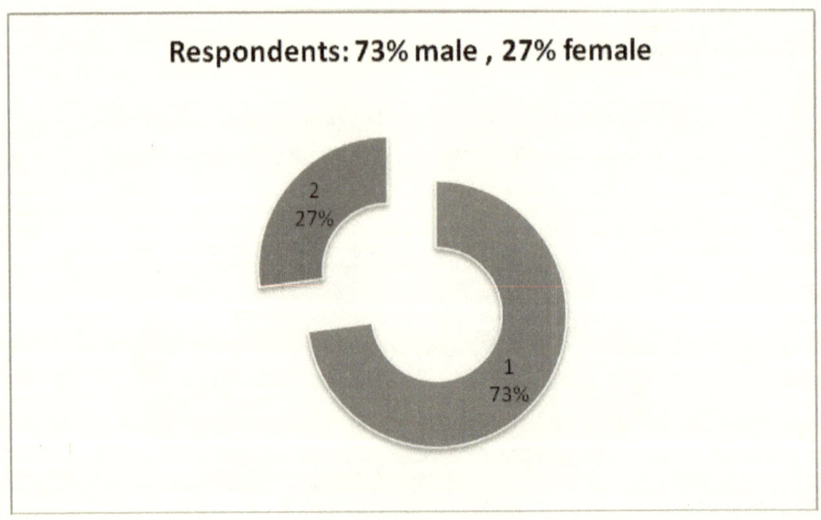

Respondents: 73% male , 27% female
2
27%
1
73%

APPENDIX

64% age 31 to 45, 23% age 21 to 30 years
64
36
1
2

Education level
Sec to NITEC
18%
Master
27%
Diploma
10%
Bachelor
45%

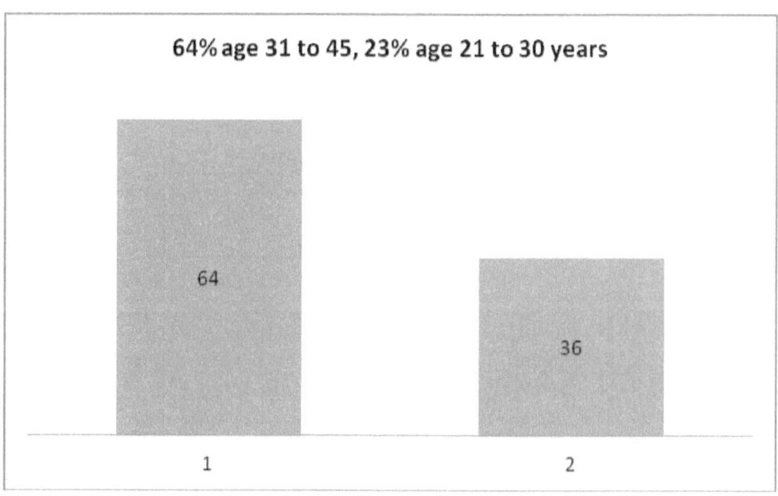

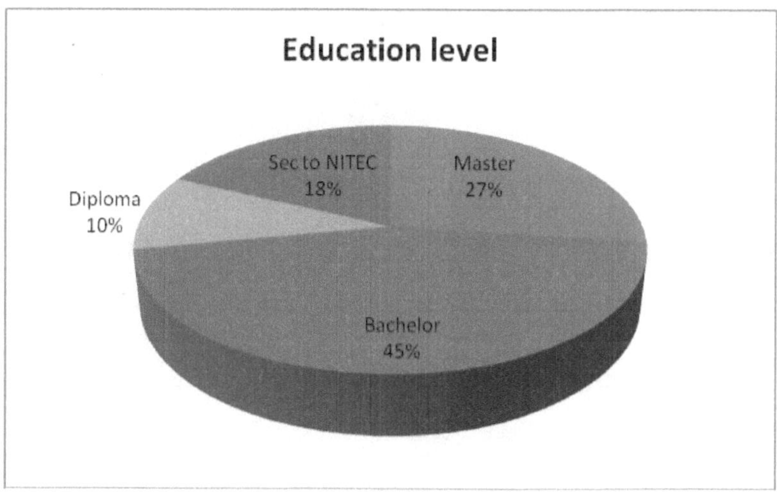

Cronbach's Alpha	Internal Rate of Consistency
a = 1.0	Perfect
a> / = .9	Excellent
a> / = .8	Good
a> / = .7	Acceptable
a> / = .6	Questionable
a> / = .5	Poor
a < 0.5	Unacceptable

APPENDIX 1 SAMPLE

Name: XXXXXX

Occupation: Auxiliary Police

DOB: 15/05/73

Highest Education: NTC-2, Advanced Cert in Security Supervision

Evaluating the opportunity for growth in the Business for Security Industry in Singapore

Open ended questionnaire. The information will be used for Academic research purposes only.

1) **In your view, is the Security industry constantly in demand of manpower?**

   If:

In my view, it is constantly in demand, due to the requirements of part time officers, and the buffering for the relief. There are many times for instance, auxiliary police officers are on MCs, the need for either part time or relief will be necessary. Even in the unarmed sector, the officers are constantly on Medical leaves; therefore relief is very much needed. With ample budgeting, extra officers are used as a form of buffering to help in the security duties.

2) **Do you think that the tightening of standard by the PLRD over the years has improved the standard of the security professional (Security guards/protection officers/security officers) to effectively handle security and counter-terrorism situation?**

It is good for PLRD to improve the standards of the security professionals, as to prepare the officers for any worst case scenarios in security issues, and there should never be complacency in handling security issues, therefore I would say 'Yes', it has improved the standard over the years.

3) **In general, do you think local young Singaporeans will consider a career in the Security Industry?**

If you talk specifically into the Auxiliary Police Force Sector, I would think it's yes, but to a certain extent. It is possible due to salary and progress in certain specialized sector, such as the auxiliary police force. Generally, young Singapore may still consider. However, for unarmed sector, it will likely not be the case, due to many factors, such as low prestige and low pay, long hours.

4) **What do you think, hinder local young Singaporeans to consider a career in the security industry? (Example, would it be long hours, low pay, unproductive duties, under utilization, mundane, lack of risk etc)**

Generally, no progress in rank and getting stagnated will be the consideration deterring them to consider the career. This affects local young Singapore below the rank of Diploma, however, with a Diploma at least, rank status will rise within a couple of years.

5) **What do you think, can promote young educated Singaporeans (Diploma and above) to consider a career in the security industry? (Example, would it be better pay, shorter working hours, extra capabilities, increase prestige given to the job etc)**

Possibly with being educated, progression in rank and responsibility will be what educated local you Singaporeans will be looking into, apart from better pay, and shorter working hours.

6) **In your opinion, should Security films in Singapore have at least a couple of people who are highly experience/trained in the management of a business, so that they can help the overall enhancement of the security business?**

I would say yes, this is due to, to sustain and improve the business according to the economy. Without people who are highly educated in business or management, the tendency of the running of a business may be at a success rate of 60/40 %. I wouldn't deny that running a business need not be someone with an MBA or BBA, but however, it does help with someone who is business trained at a certain level, to help see things better, as compared to an operation veteran.

7) **In your opinion, with a better remuneration package, shorter hours provided, and stronger management, branding, and prestige built over the Security Film helps to enhance the security business, would you agree with the statement (or to some extent)?**

Yes, of course. For the sake of stability and recognition, the above all mentioned should be built comprehensively.

Thank you for your valuable feedbacks!

APPENDIX 2 SAMPLE

Name: XXXXXX

Occupation: Customer Service

DOB: 19th November 1979

Highest Education: Secondary

<u>Evaluating the opportunity for growth in the Business for Security Industry in Singapore</u>

<u>Open ended questionnaire. The information will be used for Academic research purposes only.</u>

1) **In your view, is the Security industry constantly in demand of manpower?**

   Yes, security Industry no matter where, and at which locations, will always in need of man power. This is because, it is something that we, as human beings cannot take for granted and in this society, a lot of places need security personnel to look after lives, properties and to make sure things are in order.

2) **Do you think that the tightening of standard by the PLRD over the years has improved the standard of the**

security   professional   (Security   guards/protection officers/security officers) to effectively handle security and counter-terrorism situation?

I agree that the PLRD has tightened and improved the standard of security personnel over the years, because no matter in which industry, there is always room for improvement and by tightening the standard; it shows the professionalism of the people doing the job. So yes indeed, they did improved.

3) In general, do you think local young Singaporeans will consider a career in the Security Industry?

Young Singaporeans will consider security as a job due to many reasons, such as having the interest to work part time in short term, that is to make easy money for events. Another reason would be some may be unable to find a good job; therefore security takes in people easily. There are also those formerly from various uniform groups, who are interested in this line, and there is no need to be train for these group of former personnel, therefore this job suits them. However, they would still need to update the PLRD for courses and self- development over time.

4) **What do you think, hinder local young Singaporeans to consider a career in the security industry? (Example, would it be long hours, low pay, unproductive duties, under utilization, mundane, lack of risk etc)**

Like in any industry, there is bound to have people being unhappy able their jobs, which are also due to a number of reasons. Security jobs, especially in a more regimental setting, with VIP clients or demanding requirements, will have a lot of stress in works directly. The nature of job scopes, low pay in most security firms, long working hours, and stress contributes to the concentration and fatigue level.

5) **What do you think, can promote young educated Singaporeans (Diploma and above) to consider a career in the security industry? (Example, would it be better pay, shorter working hours, extra capabilities, increase prestige given to the job etc)**

Security Industry like most service industry had the least respect in terms of jobs status. This may be due to a lot of people looking down at the job. There also also various negative reasons, like stress in works due to nature of job scopes, low pay in most security firms, long working hours, thus unable to concentrate. But there is always room for improvements like better pay, shorter working hours, and increase prestige given to the job.

Thank you for your valuable feedbacks!

APPENDIX 3 SAMPLE

Name: XXXXXX

Occupation: SELF DEFENSE INSTRUCTOR

DOB: 8 SEP 1973

Highest Education: BUSINESS DEGREE

Evaluating the opportunity for growth in the Business for Security Industry in Singapore

Open ended questionnaire. The information will be used for Academic research purposes only.

1) **In your view, is the Security industry constantly in demand of manpower?**

   Yes. This mainly due to the perceived low status and low pay that security officers get. They are not able to retain young people and often can only get the elderly or retired to work. Turnover is quite high and job satisfaction is low. This couple of aspects I mentioned, has indeed, created the demand of manpower. It would seem more like a negative reason for demand than good.

2) Do you think that the tightening of standard by the PLRD over the years has improved the standard of the security professional (Security guards/protection officers/security officers) to effectively handle security and counter-terrorism situation?

I wouldn't be sure, but I would say that no matter what, the tightening, and increase certification does help improved the overall standard of security professionals in some way. It is like a more 'trained' person will likely perform better or proper, as compared to a 'non trained' personnel, who would be deemed as 'rookie'.

3) In general, do you think local young Singaporeans will consider a career in the Security Industry?

Currently, due to the high level of living in Singapore, it is still "safer' to choose the better paying jobs over the lower end (salary wise) and more 'dangerous' jobs like security. However there are people who do choose this path but they are more likely the minority. The lack of status is another factor. Younger people do not like to be looked down or get teased by fellow peers when it comes to career choices.

4) **What do you think, hinder local young Singaporeans to consider a career in the security industry? (Example, would it be long hours, low pay, unproductive duties, under utilization, mundane, lack of risk etc)**

The main factors are low pay, low status and the uncertainty of where it will lead one's career. No one, who could secure a better pay elsewhere, would settle for a lower pay job, unless it proves to be more job satisfying by layman perception. The low status would also be the good reason, and the uncertainty of prospect or promotion would be a good deterrence.

5) **What do you think, can promote young educated Singaporeans (Diploma and above) to consider a career in the security industry? (Example, would it be better pay, shorter working hours, extra capabilities, increase prestige given to the job etc)**

The first thing is 'Better pay'. Somehow, if the status can be built to increase to a level of professionalism and elitism, it will entice the group of either sport, martial arts trained, highly educated, or former high ranking officers in the government forces to join.

6) **In your opinion, should Security films in Singapore have at least a couple of people who are highly experience/trained in the management of a business, so that they can help the overall enhancement of the security business?**

That will be preferred by more often than not, but usually, smaller security film run on low budget, therefore standard of running is low, and competition can be cut throat, which is why the film would rather not get people who are highly educated in business administration, but not in the industry before.

7) **In your opinion, with a better remuneration package, shorter hours provided, and stronger management, branding, and prestige built over the Security Film helps to enhance the security business, would you agree with the statement (or to some extent)?**

Yes, because those mentioned are the very main reasons lacked, that people do not choose to be a security officer.

Thank you for your valuable feedbacks!

APPENDIX 4 SAMPLE

<u>Evaluating the opportunity for growth in the Business for Security Industry in Singapore</u>

<u>Please take about 10 minutes to fill up this close/open ended questionnaire. The information will be used for Academic research purposes only.</u>

1) **If you were to be given a chance to see yourself in a security (Protection Officer/Security Officer/ Security Guard) job, what do you think will be the 'likes' and 'dislike' ? Please rate 1 to 5, with 1 the best, while 5 the worst.**

   Salary: 1, 2, 3, 4, 5   (Answer here____3___)

   Working hours (Average 10 to 12 working hours): 1, 2, 3, 4, 5   (Answer here___2___)

   Job satisfaction: 1, 2, 3, 4, 5   (Answer here___3___)

   Job status: 1, 2, 3, 4, 5   (Answer here__3___)

   Productivity: 1, 2, 3, 4, 5   (Answer here___3___)

2) **In your personal opinion, which of the following (working hours, salary, productivity, status or etc) do you think, needed great improvement to help attract younger and higher educated (Diploma and above) to consider a security (Protection Officer/Security Officer/ Security Guard) job?**

(Please comment in some sentences)

Everyone works for money. So, the remuneration package needs to be attractive. And younger people also want to have more learning opportunities and better career prospects.

3) **The security business in Singapore is sustainable.**

If:

Yes (why do you think so?), But may need more foreigners, if the take up rate by locals is low, due to unattractive remuneration, prospects and long working hours.

No____ (Why do you think so?)

Not sure

4) **The security industry in Singapore has the potential opportunity for growth.**

If:

Yes (Why?), provided more is done, to make it more attractive for younger people.

No____(Why?)

Not sure

5) **Despite the prevalent terrorism attacks around the world, Singapore will need enough Security manpower to safeguard the residential and commercial buildings alike.**

Strongly Agree

Agree   ✓

Disagree

Strongly   Disagree   (If   strongly   disagree,   why?)

____

6) **In your opinion, a Security Officer's job is:**

Redundant to have

Imperative to have   ✓

Good to have

Not necessary

7) **In your opinion, you view a security officer's job as (Underline your rating):**

Redundant – Strongly Agree, Agree, Neutral, <u>Disagree</u>, Strongly Disagree

Unproductive – Strongly Agree, Agree, Neutral, <u>Disagree</u>, Strongly Disagree

Embarrassing – Strongly Agree, Agree, Neutral, <u>Disagree</u>, Strongly Disagree

Low end in nature – Strongly Agree, Agree, <u>Neutral</u>, Disagree, Strongly Disagree

8) **Imagine yourself as a security officer standing guard against theft in a shopping mall in the midst of the public, you will likely feel (Underline your rating):**

Redundant – Strongly Agree, Agree, <u>Neutral</u>, Disagree, Strongly Disagree

Unproductive – Strongly Agree, Agree, <u>Neutral</u>, Disagree, Strongly Disagree

Embarrassing – Strongly Agree, _Agree_, Neutral, Disagree, Strongly Disagree

Low end in nature – Strongly Agree, _Agree_, Neutral, Disagree, Strongly Disagree

9) **In view of enhancing the capabilities of a Security officer/Guard, a Security Officer/Guard should be trained in self-defence skills/unarmed combat related:**

Strongly Agree ✓

Agree

Disagree

Strongly Disagree

If 'Strongly Agree' or 'Agree', please proceed to question 10, and then question 12. If 'Disagree or 'Strongly Disagree', please proceed to question 11, and then question 12.

10) **If you have stated 'strongly agree' or 'agree', which of the 3 out of 8 self-defence skills do you think can best equip a Security officer/Guard to enhance his/her physical defence capability?**

Please choose and type in rank '1', '2'   '3' beside the selected skills:

Karate (Japanese art of empty hand fighting) _____

Taekwondo (Korean art of self-defence) _________

Muay Thai (Thai kick boxing) ________

Krav Maga (Israeli Military Forces Self Defence) ___2_____

MMA (Mixed martial arts consisting of muay thai, jiu jitsu etc) _____3__

Wing Chun (Bruce Lee's first art of self-defence derived from IP Man, for close battle) _____1_

Judo (Japanese art of throws and ground defence) _______________

11) **IF you have felt that s Security Officer/Guard do not need to acquire any physical defence skills, please comment why not?**

____

12) **The Security Industry Regulatory Authority has made known that self-defence training is not necessary to be acquired by Security Officers/Guard (as they are to be utilized only to watch, deter, and report when necessary). Do you agree totally?**

If:

Yes. Please comment ____

No. Please comment: To watch? Deter? So, basically, only eye power and mouth power? In cases of real crisis, how will these be sufficient to help?

13) **Despite the hiring and outsourcing needs for physical security, the Security Industry in Singapore will have the opportunity for growth in the coming years.**

Strongly Agree

Agree   ✓

Disagree

Strongly Disagree (If strongly disagree, why?)

Name: XXXXX 1

Occupation: self-employed

DOB: 30/03/76

Highest Education: Diploma

Thank you for your valuable feedbacks!

APPENDIX 5 SAMPLE

Evaluating the opportunity for growth in the Business for Security Industry in Singapore

Please take about 10 minutes to fill up this close/open ended questionnaire. The information will be used for Academic research purposes only.

8) **If you were to be given a chance to see yourself in a security (Protection Officer/Security Officer/ Security Guard) job, what do you think will be the 'likes' and 'dislike' ? Please rate 1 to 5, with 1 the best, while 5 the worst.**

   Salary: 1, 2, 3, 4, 5   (Answer here___5___)

   Working hours (Average 10 to 12 working hours): 1, 2, 3, 4, 5   (Answer here___5___)

   Job satisfaction: 1, 2, 3, 4, 5   (Answer here___5___)

   Job status: 1, 2, 3, 4, 5   (Answer here___5___)

   Productivity: 1, 2, 3, 4, 5   (Answer here___5___)

9) **Open ended question:**

   In your personal opinion, which of the following (working hours, salary, productivity, status or etc) do you think, needed great improvement to help attract younger and higher educated (Diploma and above) to consider a security (Protection Officer/Security Officer/ Security Guard) job?

- An improvement to career prospects. Such as providing young educated people with greater responsibilities and roles. A career path towards higher management.

(Please comment in some sentences)

10) The security business in Singapore is sustainable.

If:

No: large in-flux of foreigners who can readily be trained to take on the role. The demand for protecting physical assets may be depleting as compared to digital/cyber assets.

11) The security industry in Singapore has the potential opportunity for growth.

If:

Not sure

12) Despite the prevalent terrorism attacks around the world, Singapore will need enough Security manpower to safeguard the residential and commercial buildings alike.

Fairly Agree to a certain extend

13) In your opinion, a Security Officer's job is:

Good to have

14) In your opinion, you view a security officer's job as (Underline your rating):

Redundant – Strongly Agree, Agree, <u>Neutral</u>, Disagree, Strongly Disagree

Unproductive – <u>Strongly Agree</u>, Agree, Neutral, Disagree, Strongly Disagree

Embarrassing – Strongly Agree, Agree, Neutral, <u>Disagree</u>, Strongly Disagree

Low end/skilled in nature – Strongly Agree, Agree, Neutral, <u>Disagree</u>, Strongly Disagree

15) **Imagine yourself as a security officer standing guard against theft in a shopping mall in the midst of the public, you will likely feel (Underline your rating):**

Redundant – <u>Strongly Agree</u>, Agree, Neutral, Disagree, Strongly Disagree

Unproductive – <u>Strongly Agree</u>, Agree, Neutral, Disagree, Strongly Disagree

Embarrassing – Strongly Agree, <u>Agree</u>, Neutral, Disagree, Strongly Disagree

Low end in nature – Strongly Agree, <u>Agree</u>, Neutral, Disagree, Strongly Disagree

16) **In view of enhancing the capabilities of a Security officer/Guard, a Security Officer/Guard should be trained in self-defence skills/unarmed combat related:**

Agree

If 'Strongly Agree' or 'Agree', please proceed to question 10, and then question 12. If 'Disagree or 'Strongly Disagree', please proceed to question 11, and then question 12.

17) If you have stated 'strongly agree' or 'agree', which of the 3 out of 8 self-defence skills do you think can best equip a Security officer/Guard to enhance his/her physical defence capability?

Please choose and type in rank '1', '2' '3' beside the selected skills:

Karate (Japanese art of empty hand fighting) ____

Taekwondo (Korean art of self-defence) 3

Muay Thai (Thai kick boxing) _______

Krav Maga (Israeli Military Forces Self Defence) 2

MMA (Mixed martial arts consisting of muay thai, jiu jitsu etc) 1

Wing Chun (Bruce Lee's first art of self-defence derived from IP Man, for close battle) _____

Judo (Japanese art of throws and ground defence)

18) IF you have felt that s Security Officer/Guard do not need to acquire any physical defence skills, please comment why not?

____

19) **The Security Industry Regulatory Authority has made known that self-defence training is not necessary to be acquired by Security Officers/Guard (as they are to be utilized only to watch, deter, and report when necessary). Do you agree totally?**

If:

No. In the event of a threat to public safety and assets, the security officer is the first touch point to mitigate such risks. S/he should be expected to be competent in some basic combat / self-defense skills to handle such situations should it arise.

20) **Despite the hiring and outsourcing needs for physical security, the Security Industry in Singapore will have the opportunity for growth in the coming years.**

Disagree

Name: XXXXX

Occupation: Public Servant

DOB: 11 Sep 1984

Highest Education: Master

Thank you for your valuable feedbacks!

APPENDIX 6 SAMPLE

Evaluating the opportunity for growth in the Business for Security Industry in Singapore

Please take about 10 minutes to fill up this close/open ended questionnaire. The information will be used for Academic research purposes only.

1) **If you were to be given a chance to see yourself in a security (Protection Officer/Security Officer/ Security Guard) job, what do you think will be the 'likes' and 'dislike' ? Please rate 1 to 5, with 1 the best, while 5 the worst.**

   Salary: 1, 2, 3, 4, 5   (Answer here___4___)

   Working hours (Average 10 to 12 working hours): 1, 2, 3, 4, 5   (Answer here __5___)

   Job satisfaction: 1, 2, 3, 4, 5   (Answer here___4___)

   Job status: 1, 2, 3, 4, 5   (Answer here___5___)

   Productivity: 1, 2, 3, 4, 5   (Answer here___4___)

2) **In your personal opinion, which of the following (working hours, salary, productivity, status or etc) do**

you think, needed great improvement to help attract younger and higher educated (Diploma and above) to consider a security (Protection Officer/Security Officer/ Security Guard) job?

(Please comment in some sentences) Status needs great improvement because young locals with higher education definitely do not want to work for a job that only requires o'level education.

3) **The security business in Singapore is sustainable.**

If:

Yes ______Because industries will definitely need security guards, protection officers, they cannot be replaced by machines or robots. (Why do you think so?)

No_______________________________________ (Why do you think so?)

Not sure_____________________

4) **The security industry in Singapore has the potential opportunity for growth.**

If:

Yes _________________________________ (Why?)

No______________________________________(Why?)

Not sure ____Currently, i feel there isnt any opportunity for growth because the no., of security workers needed for an industry is usually fixed in my impression unless there is an increase no. of crime rates in Singapore.____________

5) **Despite the prevalent terrorism attacks around the world, Singapore will need enough Security manpower to safeguard the residential and commercial buildings alike.**

<u>Strongly Agree</u>

Agree

Disagree

Strongly Disagree (If strongly disagree, why?)

____

6) **In your opinion, a Security Officer's job is:**

Redundant to have

Imperative to have

<u>Good to have</u>

Not necessary

7) **In your opinion, you view a security officer's job as (Underline your rating):**

Redundant – Strongly Agree, Agree, Neutral, Disagree, <u>Strongly Disagree</u>

Unproductive – Strongly Agree, <u>Agree</u>, Neutral, Disagree, Strongly Disagree

Embarrassing – Strongly Agree, Agree, <u>Neutral</u>, Disagree, Strongly Disagree

Low end in nature – Strongly Agree, <u>Agree</u>, Neutral, Disagree, Strongly Disagree

8) **Imagine yourself as a security officer standing guard against theft in a shopping mall in the midst of the public, you will likely feel (Underline your rating):**

Redundant – Strongly Agree, <u>Agree</u>, Neutral, Disagree, Strongly Disagree

Unproductive – Strongly Agree, Agree, <u>Neutral,</u> Disagree, Strongly Disagree

Embarrassing – Strongly Agree, <u>Agree</u>, Neutral, Disagree, Strongly Disagree

Low end in nature – Strongly Agree, <u>Agree</u>, Neutral, Disagree, Strongly Disagree

9) In view of enhancing the capabilities of a Security officer/Guard, a Security Officer/Guard should be trained in self-defence skills/unarmed combat related:

<u>Strongly Agree</u>

Agree

Disagree

Strongly Disagree

If 'Strongly Agree' or 'Agree', please proceed to question 10, and then question 12. If 'Disagree or 'Strongly Disagree', please proceed to question 11, and then question 12.

10) If you have stated 'strongly agree' or 'agree', which of the 3 out of 8 self-defence skills do you think can best equip a Security officer/Guard to enhance his/her physical defence capability?

Please choose and type in rank '1', '2' '3' beside the selected skills:

Karate (Japanese art of empty hand fighting) _____

Taekwondo (Korean art of self-defence) ________-

Muay Thai (Thai kick boxing) _______

Krav Maga (Israeli Military Forces Self Defence) ___1____

MMA (Mixed martial arts consisting of muay thai, jiu jitsu etc) _______

Wing Chun (Bruce Lee's first art of self-defence derived from IP Man, for close battle) __3____

Judo (Japanese art of throws and ground defence) __2__

11) **IF you have felt that a Security Officer/Guard do not need to acquire any physical defence skills, please comment why not?**

____

____

12) **The Security Industry Regulatory Authority has made known that self-defence training is not necessary to be acquired by Security Officers/Guard (as they are to be utilized only to watch, deter, and report when necessary). Do you agree totally?**

If:

Yes. Please comment ________________________________

No. Please comment: Security officers should be trained in self-defence training because when crisis happens, security officers need to be armed with self-defence tactics to prevent themselves from getting hurt. It will be too late if they inform the police officers to fight off.

13) Despite the hiring and outsourcing needs for physical security, the Security Industry in Singapore will have the opportunity for growth in the coming years.

Strongly Agree

Agree

Disagree

Strongly Disagree (If strongly disagree, why?)

Name: XXXXXX

Occupation: Admin Assistant

DOB: 9th January 1986

Highest Education: Bachelor Degree

Thank you for your valuable feedbacks!

ABOUT THE AUTHOR

Kenray Tan began his first career in the armed security industry protecting the properties of 2 Cabinet VVIP, after serving his national service as an SAF Commando. A few years later, he moved on to the private education industry, playing roles such as the examination administrator, lecturer management senior executive, student development trainer, lecturer development training senior executive, and student care service senior facilitator. He acquired skills in the area of Curriculum, Assessment, Training, and Pedagogy, before answering the call to revert to his current role as a security professional. His propensity and radical interest in security, Special Forces, counter-terrorism, terrorism, strategic studies, and political science led him to a management role in the security industry, managing a cluster and operations of approximately 50 personnel. Being passionate in the industry and being one of the higher academically qualified personnel, Kenray's vision is to bring the security industry in Singapore to a greater height and that the status of each individual security officer is raised.

Apart from Security, Kenray holds an SKF first degree black belt in Karate more than a decade ago and in recent years, another first degree black belt in Shotokan Karate. He had taught karate to various organizations previously. He was also trained in Police Defence Tactics, Police Unarmed Tactics, Israeli's KAPAP, Taekwondo Gym, Unarmed Combat, and attended a seminar in Krav Maga, Jeet Kune Do, Capoeira, Kali weapon, Yang Tai Chi, Muay Thai fitness, Torchlight Self Defence, and Russian Martial Arts Systema. He is CPR certified, as well as attended a course in defensive driving. He also holds a WDA cert in People Protection service, which allows him to execute executive/close protection, amid other security modules he has taken and will be taking in future to enhance his capability for the work in the industry.

In Academic, Kenray holds a Master of Science in Management Degree from University College Dublin, National University of Ireland – a Triple Crown Accredited University for Business Faculty, with a Research Paper on the Security industry in Singapore. He also holds a Bachelor of Communications Degree (PR, Crisis Management, Advertising, Integrate Marcom etc) from Edith Cowan University, Perth, Western Australia, Advanced Diploma in Mass Communications, Advanced Diploma in Business Management, and a Diploma in Marketing from a Management Institution.

In training and teaching, Kenray holds a full Advanced Certificate in Training and Assessment (ACTA) qualification for WDA competency training and assessment as a potential trainer, Cambridge International Diploma for Teachers and Trainers (CIDTT) for private teaching, RP Specialist Diploma in Applied Learning and Teaching (SDALT) for private lecturing, and a UK teacher certificate in public speaking. He also achieved certificates online, such as 'Understanding Research Methods' from University of London, 'Public Relation Research' from National University of Singapore, and 'Terrorism and Counter-Terrorism, comparing theory and practice' from Leiden University through Coursera platform, and 'How to Survive your PHD' from Australia National University through EDX platform, all for his personal development. He looks forward to keeping himself learnt along the years of his lifetime. He can be reached via email at lloydtan@singnet.com.sg or elite_agent84@yahoo.com.sg

Facebook page: Security and Counter-Terrorism Watch

Below is a range of certificates he had achieved, but not limited to, as a life-long learner:

<u>Security and Military related but not limited to:</u>

1) WDA Provide People Protection Certificate (Bodyguard)

2) WDA Handle Counter-Terrorism Activities Certificate (HCTA)

3) WDA Crowd and Traffic Control Certificate

4) WDA Conduct Security Screening of Person and Bag

5) WDA Provide Safety and Security (F1)

6) 185th BAC (Basic Airborne Course) Certificate of completion

7) Commando Signaller Vocation Certificate of completion

8) Army Logistic Armskote Certificate of attendance

9) Defensive Driving Course Certificate of Attendance

10) CPR + AED Certification

11) Indoor Skydiving Participation certificate

12) Arizona Concealed Handgun safety certificate

13) Terrorism and Counter-Terrorism, Comparing Theory and Practice – Leiden University @Coursera

14) Member – International Association for Counter-Terrorism and Security Personnel

15) PWM Senior Security Supervisor

16) Police officer Basic Course

Martial Arts and Sports Related:

1) First Degree Black Belt Shitoryu Karate Certificate 2002 - Civil Defence 2nd Division HQ

2) First Degree Black Belt grading letter 2004 - Singapore Karate Federation

3) For National Squad centralised training for Karate - Former Trainee

4) Taken part in Pesta Sukan, National Junior and Cadet Tournament, and Inter-Club Tournament and won some medals

5) Brown tip - Singapore Taekwondo Gymnasium - 2007

6) Escrima/Kali weapon workshop certificate in 2005 - Kuen Culture

7) Jeet Kune Do workshop certificate in 2005 - Kuen Culture

8) Israeli Special Force Krav Panim Al Panim (KAPAP) workshops Certificate for completion in 2010 - SAFRA Jurong

9) National Coaching Accreditation Program (NCAP) Theory level 1 certificate

10) National Coaching Accreditation Program (NCAP) Karate Technical level 1 certificate

11) National Coaching Accreditation Program (NCAP) Theory level 2 certificate

12) Krav Maga Global (KMG) Seminar Certificate of participation in 2013

13) Instructor - Singapore Police Force's Martial Arts Control Unit (MACU), until law repeals in 2005, and then martial arts was introduced and evolved as sports in Singapore, which the MACU instructor license pathway was diverted to coaching certifications by the Singapore Sports Council.

14) Shotokan International Karate First Dan certificate - 2013

15) National Physical Fitness and Assessment (NAPFA) Certificate - 2005

16) SNCS Rockclimbing level 1 – 2003

17) ISKA – Kickboxing Instructor Certificate – 2015

Education and Training:

1) UCD-NUID Master of Science in Management

2) ECU Bachelor of Communications (Communications Management)

3) RP Specialist Diploma in Applied learning and Teaching

4) Cambridge International Diploma for Teachers and Trainer

5) Advanced Certificate in Training and Assessment

6) Advanced Diploma in Business Management

7) Advanced Diploma in Mass Communications

8) Diploma in Marketing

9) Educare Kagan Cooperative learning Pedagogy Certificate

10) MDIS Classroom Management Workshop Certificate

11) NIE Dissertation/ Thesis Supervision Certificate

12) College of Teachers UK London, Certificate in Public Speaking

13) Understanding your Research – University of London @Coursera

14) Public Relations Research – National University of Singapore @Coursera

15) Surviving your PHD – Australia National University @EDX

16) Member – Mensa Society Singapore

17) Member – Association of Professional Trainers

www.ingramcontent.com/pod-product-compliance
Lightning Source LLC
Chambersburg PA
CBHW030314160726
47992CB00005B/2005